HAITIAN IMMIGRATION

Jena Gaines

THE CHANGING Face of North America:
IMMIGRATION SINCE 1965

HAITIAN IMMIGRATION

Jena Gaines

MASON CREST PUBLISHERS
PHILADELPHIA

Produced by OTTN Publishing, Stockton, New Jersey

Mason Crest Publishers
370 Reed Road
Broomall, PA 19008
www.masoncrest.com

First printing

1 3 5 7 9 8 6 4 2

Library of Congress Cataloging-in-Publication Data

Gaines, Jena.
  Haitian immigration / Jena Gaines.
    p.   cm. — (The changing face of North America)
Summary: An overview of immigration from Haiti to the United States and Canada since the 1960s, discussing
conditions leading to emigration, cultural adjustments and problems facing immigrants, and more.
Includes bibliographical references (p.) and index.
  ISBN 1-59084-691-5
1. Haitian Americans—History—20th century—Juvenile literature. 2. Haitians—Canada—History—20th
century—Juvenile literature. 3. Immigrants—United States—History—20th century—Juvenile literature.
4. Immigrants—Canada—History—20th century—Juvenile literature. Haiti—Emigration and immigration—
History—20th century—Juvenile literature. 6. United States—Emigration and immigration—History—20th
century—Juvenile literature. 7. Canada—Emigration and immigration—History—20th century—Juvenile
literature. [1. Haiti—Emigration and immigration. 2. United States—Emigration and immigration. 3. Canada—
Emigration and immigration. 4. Haitian Americans. 5. Haitians—Canada. 6. Immigrants.] I. Title. II. Series.
E184.H27 G35 2004
304.8'7307294—dc22

                                                                                      2003018382

THE **CHANGING**
Face of North America:
IMMIGRATION SINCE 1965

CONTENTS

INTRODUCTION

THE CHANGING FACE OF AMERICA

By Senator Edward M. Kennedy

America is proud of its heritage and history as a nation of immigrants, and my own family is an example. All eight of my great-grandparents were immigrants who left Ireland a century and a half ago, when that land was devastated by the massive famine caused by the potato blight. When I was a young boy, my grandfather used to take me down to the docks in Boston and regale me with stories about the Great Famine and the waves of Irish immigrants who came to America seeking a better life. He talked of how the Irish left their marks in Boston and across the nation, enduring many hardships and harsh discrimination, but also building the railroads, digging the canals, settling the West, and filling the factories of a growing America. According to one well-known saying of the time, "under every railroad tie, an Irishman is buried."

America was the promised land for them, as it has been for so many other immigrants who have found shelter, hope, opportunity, and freedom. Immigrants have always been an indispensable part of our nation. They have contributed immensely to our communities, created new jobs and whole new industries, served in our armed forces, and helped make America the continuing land of promise that it is today.

The inspiring poem by Emma Lazarus, inscribed on the pedestal of the Statue of Liberty in New York Harbor, is America's welcome to all immigrants:

Give me your tired, your poor,
Your huddled masses yearning to breathe free,
The wretched refuse of your teeming shore,
Send these, the homeless, tempest-tossed, to me:
I lift my lamp beside the golden door.

The period since September 11, 2001, has been particularly challenging for immigrants. Since the horrifying terrorist attacks, there has been a resurgence of anti-immigrant attitudes and behavior. We all agree that our borders must be safe and secure. Yet, at the same time, we must safeguard the entry of the millions of persons who come to the United States legally each year as immigrants, visitors, scholars, students, and workers. The "golden door" must stay open. We must recognize that immigration is not the problem—terrorism is. We must identify and isolate the terrorists, and not isolate America.

One of my most important responsibilities in the Senate is the preservation of basic rights and basic fairness in the application of our immigration laws, so that new generations of immigrants in our own time and for all time will have the same opportunity that my great-grandparents had when they arrived in America.

Immigration is beneficial for the United States and for countries throughout the world. It is no coincidence that two hundred years ago, our nations' founders chose *E Pluribus Unum*—"out of many, one"—as America's motto. These words, chosen by Benjamin Franklin, John Adams, and Thomas Jefferson, refer to the ideal that separate colonies can be transformed into one united nation. Today, this ideal has come to apply to individuals as well. Our diversity is our strength. We are a nation of immigrants, and we always will be.

FOREWORD

THE CHANGING FACE OF THE UNITED STATES

Marian L. Smith, historian
U.S. Immigration and Naturalization Service

Americans commonly assume that immigration today is very different than immigration of the past. The immigrants themselves appear to be unlike immigrants of earlier eras. Their language, their dress, their food, and their ways seem strange. At times people fear too many of these new immigrants will destroy the America they know. But has anything really changed? Do new immigrants have any different effect on America than old immigrants a century ago? Is the American fear of too much immigration a new development? Do immigrants really change America more than America changes the immigrants? The very subject of immigration raises many questions.

In the United States, immigration is more than a chapter in a history book. It is a continuous thread that links the present moment to the first settlers on North American shores. From the first colonists' arrival until today, immigrants have been met by Americans who both welcomed and feared them. Immigrant contributions were always welcome—on the farm, in the fields, and in the factories. Welcoming the poor, the persecuted, and the "huddled masses" became an American principle. Beginning with the original Pilgrims' flight from religious persecution in the 1600s, through the Irish migration to escape starvation in the 1800s, to the relocation of Central Americans seeking refuge from civil wars in the 1980s and 1990s, the United States has considered itself a haven for the destitute and the oppressed.

But there was also concern that immigrants would not adopt American ways, habits, or language. Too many immigrants might overwhelm America. If so, the dream of the Founding Fathers for United States government and society would be destroyed. For this reason, throughout American history some have argued that limiting or ending immigration is our patriotic duty. Benjamin Franklin feared there were so many German immigrants in Pennsylvania the Colonial Legislature would begin speaking German. "Progressive" leaders of the early 1900s feared that immigrants who could not read and understand the English language were not only exploited by "big business," but also served as the foundation for "machine politics" that undermined the U.S. Constitution. This theme continues today, usually voiced by those who bear no malice toward immigrants but who want to preserve American ideals.

Have immigrants changed? In colonial days, when most colonists were of English descent, they considered Germans, Swiss, and French immigrants as different. They were not "one of us" because they spoke a different language. Generations later, Americans of German or French descent viewed Polish, Italian, and Russian immigrants as strange. They were not "like us" because they had a different religion, or because they did not come from a tradition of constitutional government. Recently, Americans of Polish or Italian descent have seen Nicaraguan, Pakistani, or Vietnamese immigrants as too different to be included. It has long been said of American immigration that the latest ones to arrive usually want to close the door behind them.

It is important to remember that fear of individual immigrant groups seldom lasted, and always lessened. Benjamin Franklin's anxiety over German immigrants disappeared after those immigrants' sons and daughters helped the nation gain independence in the Revolutionary War. The Irish of the mid-1800s were among the most hated immigrants, but today we all wear green on St. Patrick's Day. While a century ago it was feared that Italian and other Catholic immigrants would vote as directed by the Pope, today that controversy is only a vague memory. Unfortunately, some ethnic groups continue their efforts to earn acceptance. The African

Americans' struggle continues, and some Asian Americans, whose families have been in America for generations, are the victims of current anti-immigrant sentiment.

Time changes both immigrants and America. Each wave of new immigrants, with their strange language and habits, eventually grows old and passes away. Their American-born children speak English. The immigrants' grandchildren are completely American. The strange foods of their ancestors—spaghetti, baklava, hummus, or tofu—become common in any American restaurant or grocery store. Much of what the immigrants brought to these shores is lost, principally their language. And what is gained becomes as American as St. Patrick's Day, Hanukkah, or Cinco de Mayo, and we forget that it was once something foreign.

Recent immigrants are all around us. They come from every corner of the earth to join in the American Dream. They will continue to help make the American Dream a reality, just as all the immigrants who came before them have done.

THE CHANGING FACE OF CANADA

Peter A. Hammerschmidt
First Secretary, Permanent Mission of Canada to the United Nations

Throughout Canada's history, immigration has shaped and defined the very character of Canadian society. The migration of peoples from every part of the world into Canada has profoundly changed the way we look, speak, eat, and live. Through close and distant relatives who left their lands in search of a better life, all Canadians have links to immigrant pasts. We are a nation built by and of immigrants.

Two parallel forces have shaped the history of Canadian immigration. The enormous diversity of Canada's immigrant population is the most obvious. In the beginning came the enterprising settlers of the "New World," the French and English colonists. Soon after came the Scottish, Irish, and Northern and Central European farmers of the 1700s and 1800s. As the country expanded westward during the mid-1800s, migrant workers began arriving from China, Japan, and other Asian countries. And the turbulent twentieth century brought an even greater variety of immigrants to Canada, from the Caribbean, Africa, India, and Southeast Asia.

So while English- and French-Canadians are the largest ethnic groups in the country today, neither group alone represents a majority of the population. A large and vibrant multicultural mix makes up the rest, particularly in Canada's major cities. Toronto, Vancouver, and Montreal alone are home to people from over 200 ethnic groups!

Less obvious but equally important in the evolution of Canadian immigration has been hope. The promise of a better life lured Europeans and Americans seeking cheap (sometimes even free) farmland. Thousands of Scots and Irish arrived to escape grinding poverty and starvation. Others came for freedom, to escape religious and political persecution. Canada has long been a haven to the world's dispossessed and disenfranchised—Dutch and German farmers cast out for their religious beliefs, black slaves fleeing the United States, and political refugees of despotic regimes in Europe, Africa, Asia, and South America.

The two forces of diversity and hope, so central to Canada's past, also shaped the modern era of Canadian immigration. Following the Second World War, Canada drew heavily on these influences to forge trailblazing immigration initiatives.

The catalyst for change was the adoption of the Canadian Bill of Rights in 1960. Recognizing its growing diversity and Canadians' changing attitudes towards racism, the government passed a federal statute barring discrimination on the grounds of race, national origin, color, religion, or sex. Effectively rejecting the discriminatory elements in Canadian immigration policy, the Bill of Rights forced the introduction of a new policy in 1962. The focus of immigration abruptly switched from national origin to the individual's potential contribution to Canadian society. The door to Canada was now open to every corner of the world.

Welcoming those seeking new hopes in a new land has also been a feature of Canadian immigration in the modern era. The focus on economic immigration has increased along with Canada's steadily growing economy, but political immigration has also been encouraged. Since 1945, Canada has admitted tens of thousands of displaced persons, including Jewish Holocaust survivors, victims of Soviet crackdowns in Hungary and Czechoslovakia, and refugees from political upheaval in Uganda, Chile, and Vietnam.

Prior to 1978, however, these political refugees were admitted as an exception to normal immigration procedures. That year, Canada revamped its refugee policy with a new Immigration Act that explicitly affirmed Canada's commitment to the resettlement of refugees from oppression. Today, the admission of refugees remains a central part of Canadian immigration law and regulations.

Amendments to economic and political immigration policy continued during the 1980s and 1990s, refining further the bold steps taken during the modern era. Together, these initiatives have turned Canada into one of the world's few truly multicultural states.

Unlike the process of assimilation into a "melting pot" of cultures, immigrants to Canada are more likely to retain their cultural identity, beliefs, and practices. This is the source of some of Canada's greatest strengths as a society. And as a truly multicultural nation, diversity is not seen as a threat to Canadian identity. Quite the contrary—diversity *is* Canadian identity.

1

HAITIANS IN
NORTH AMERICA

Haiti, a small Caribbean nation about the size of Maryland, has made a significant contribution to an increasingly multicultural North America. In 2000, according to the U.S. census, nearly 550,000 people of Haitian ancestry were living in the United States. Meanwhile, Canada's 2001 census counted more than 52,000 Haitian immigrants. In both countries, the actual number of Haitians may be considerably higher because of undocumented migrants (those living abroad without the permission of the host nation). In many cases these people try to avoid the census.

If undocumented immigration makes it impossible to determine with precision the size of the Haitian diaspora, as the community living outside their homeland is called, the estimates are rather startling. Haiti itself has a population of about 7.5 million, and some sources estimate the diaspora to constitute about one in six people of Haitian descent. Estimates by the U.S. Committee for Refugees (USCR) yield an even greater proportion—about one in five.

Of the more than 2.1 million Haitians it estimated were living abroad in 2001, the USCR believed that the United States was home to 1 million. Miami, New York City, and Boston each have more Haitian residents than any of Haiti's cities with the exception of the capital, Port-au-Prince.

One distinctive characteristic of most members of the Haitian diaspora is the intensity of their attachment to Haiti. Even

◀ Haiti is the poorest nation in the Western Hemisphere, a circumstance that has contributed to massive emigration. Estimates put the proportion of Haitians living abroad at one in six or higher. The United States and the Dominican Republic are by far the most popular destinations for Haitian migrants.

those who have never lived there consider it their home country and maintain ties with it.

But a variety of economic, social, and political factors have driven so many Haitians to leave—and stand in the way of their returning. Haiti is the poorest country in the Western Hemisphere and one of the poorest in the entire world. An estimated 80 percent of Haitians live below the poverty line. According to the U.S. Agency for International Development, per capita income in Haiti was under $400 in 2002; that means the average Haitian survives on about a dollar a day, though many make do with even less.

More than 90 percent of Haitian immigrants to Canada settle in French-speaking Quebec.

Once a lush, verdant land, Haiti has suffered large-scale envi-

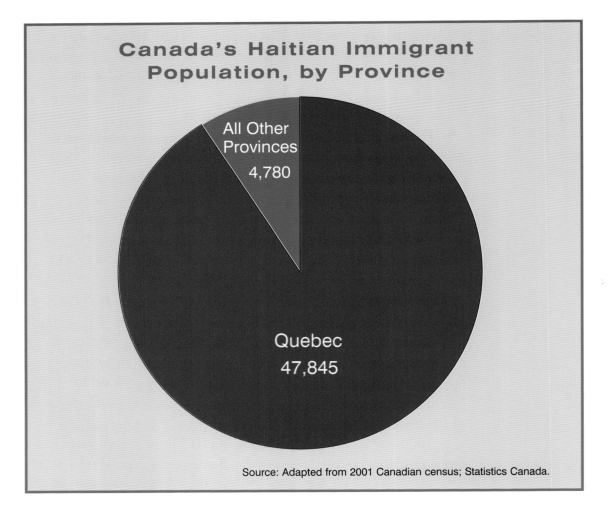

Canada's Haitian Immigrant Population, by Province

All Other Provinces
4,780

Quebec
47,845

Source: Adapted from 2001 Canadian census; Statistics Canada.

ronmental degradation: about 98 percent of the country has been deforested, which has led to massive soil erosion and made farming increasingly difficult. Each year thousands of people move from the impoverished countryside to Haiti's cities in search of jobs. Most wind up in one of the teeming slums that surround Port-au-Prince, Cap Haitien, and Gonaïves.

Educational opportunities in Haiti are very limited, particularly for the poor. About half of all Haitians cannot read or write.

In addition, Haiti's political culture has long been plagued by corruption, repression, and violence. A long-overdue experiment with democracy in 1990 was cut short the following year by a military coup. Although the military was forced to relinquish control in 1994, successive elections failed to produce political stability, as charges of electoral manipulation and outright fraud swirled. By 2004 Haiti's president clung to power, his opponents claimed, only with the help of armed gangs.

Haitians in Other Lands

In the face of these difficult circumstances, many Haitians have looked to other lands for the chance at a better life for themselves and their families. A large number—about a million, according to USCR estimates—have taken up residence in the Dominican Republic, Haiti's Spanish-speaking neighbor to the east. There they work mostly in low-paying, menial occupations. About 65,000 others have settled in the French overseas departments of Martinique, Guadeloupe, and French Guiana, where language is not an obstacle (French is one of Haiti's two official languages).

Similarly, Haitians who move to Canada are drawn to French-speaking Quebec. Of the 52,625 Haitian immigrants counted in the 2001 Canadian census, 47,845 resided in Quebec. Many arrived in one of two waves of Haitian immigration—during the 1960s and the 1980s.

Haitian immigrants came to the United States in three major waves during the last half of the 20th century: in the 1960s, the 1980s, and the 1990s. Most have settled on the East Coast.

2 A History of Strife

Hispaniola, which modern-day Haiti shares with the Dominican Republic, is the second-largest island in the Greater Antilles chain. For thousands of years before the arrival of the Europeans, indigenous tribes occupied the Caribbean island. By the 15th century, a people known as the Arawaks had settled the island, which they called Ayti, meaning "mountainous land."

Arrival of the Spanish

On December 25, 1492, during Christopher Columbus's first voyage to the New World, one of his ships, the *Santa María*, ran aground off the northwest coast of Hispaniola. Unable to fit all the sailors on the expedition onto his remaining two ships for the return voyage to Europe, Columbus left 39 men on Hispaniola and ordered them to construct a fort from the *Santa María's* timbers. The settlement, called La Navidad, was located near present-day Cap Haitien, Haiti.

When Columbus returned to Hispaniola the following year on his second expedition to the New World, he found La Navidad destroyed. All the sailors were dead, apparently killed by the Arawaks.

The Spaniards soon subdued the natives, however, forcing them to work in gold mines or on plantations that Spanish settlers established. By the 1540s warfare, disease, and overwork had reduced the native population to only a few hundred, so

◀ Police and soldiers restrain an angry crowd at the airport in Port-au-Prince, February 1986. The crowd was trying to prevent members of the hated Tonton Macoutes from escaping into exile following the collapse of Jean-Claude Duvalier's regime. Political instability and violence have continued to plague Haiti even in the post-Duvalier years.

the Spaniards began importing African slaves to perform the hard labor.

The Spanish colony was centered in the southeastern part of Hispaniola, around Santo Domingo, now the capital of the Dominican Republic. Particularly after the 16th century, Spain paid little attention to the western part of the island, and that created opportunities for settlers from other European countries.

Saint-Domingue

Over the course of the 17th century, French settlers established themselves along the northwestern and western coasts of Hispaniola. By 1697 Spain ceded the western third of the island to France according to the terms of a treaty.

The French holdings became the colony of Saint-Domingue. The colony developed into an important trade center, accounting for more than two-thirds of France's overseas trade and supplying half of the fruits and vegetables that Europeans craved.

Slavery was the engine that drove Saint-Domingue's plantation economy, and the slave system that prevailed in the colony was among the most brutal in history. Millions of Africans were brought in chains to the island and forced to work on the plantations. About half died of disease, overwork, or abuse. A slave who showed any sign of resistance was subject to whipping, branding, burning, mutilation, or other severe punishment; Saint-Domingue slaveholders could, and often did, kill those they thought were particularly troublesome.

Many French men in Saint-Domingue had children by enslaved black women. The mixed-race children of these relationships were called "mulattos." Some mulattos were legally recognized by their fathers and educated or given vocational training. The wealthiest mulattos even owned plantations and slaves of their own. Yet they were never fully accepted in white society, which viewed them as racially inferior, and they were widely resented by blacks because of the special privileges and opportunities they received.

Independence and Instability

By the late 18th century, Saint-Domingue's half-million slaves outnumbered free colonists about eight to one. Inspired by the ideals of the French Revolution, including liberty and equality, the slaves rose up against their masters in 1791. The revolt resulted in the deaths of approximately 10,000 slaves and 2,000 whites, along with widespread destruction of plantations and towns. In 1793 France was forced to outlaw slavery in the colony.

A leader of the slave revolt, Pierre Dominique Toussaint-Louverture, emerged as Saint-Domingue's political leader. He ruled with the blessing of France. After Napoleon Bonaparte became the French emperor, however, he dispatched an army to retake the Saint-Domingue colony. Although the French captured Toussaint-Louverture, they were unable to quell the resistance. Under General Jean-Jacques Dessalines, the rebels finally defeated the French army in 1803.

On January 1, 1804, the nation of Haiti officially declared its independence, with Dessalines as its leader. Haiti thus became the first free black republic in history and, after the United States, the second independent nation in the Western Hemisphere.

But political stability did

Pierre Dominique Toussaint-Louverture, a leader in the slave revolt that broke out in the Saint-Domingue colony in 1791, later ruled the entire island of Hispaniola. Though a French army succeeded in capturing Toussaint-Louverture in 1802, the French were eventually forced to withdraw, clearing the way for Haitian independence on January 1, 1804.

not follow. The assassination of Dessalines in 1806 ushered in a civil war, and rival leaders controlled the northern and southern parts of the country until Jean-Pierre Boyer reunited Haiti under his rule in 1820. A revolution drove Boyer from power in 1843, and over the next 70 years Haiti saw a total of 32 different rulers.

U.S. Intervention

During the 19th century, Haiti borrowed heavily from other countries and fell into debt. The Industrial Revolution, which transformed life in Western Europe and North America, bypassed the small Caribbean country. To make matters worse, Haiti's never-ending political and civil turmoil made businesses wary of investing in the country.

In July 1915 Haiti's president was killed by an angry mob. Around the same time, a major financial scandal came to light involving a railroad funded by German and French investors. Concerned that France or Germany—which at the time were at war with each other—might use the scandal as a pretext to occupy Haiti, U.S. president Woodrow Wilson dispatched a contingent of U.S. Marines to the country to restore order and compel the repayment of Haiti's foreign debts. Although the Americans undertook public works projects, most Haitians deeply resented the occupation, which spurred the first large migration of Haitians to the United States in the 20th century.

After the departure of the marines in 1934, Haiti experienced two decades of modest foreign investment in the country. However, the main beneficiaries of the increased economic activity were the mulatto minority, which since the early days of Haiti's independence had formed the elite of the society. Politically, Haiti remained unstable: military coups occurred in 1946, 1950, and 1956.

The Rise of Papa Doc

In 1957 national elections were held and François Duvalier became Haiti's president. A physician, Duvalier had won

The Father of American Ornithology

John James Audubon was one of the leading ornithologists and painters in the United States. His scientific and artistic studies of birds, created during the early 19th century, are still valued by historians, bird lovers, and art collectors.

Until recently, however, there was little reliable information about Audubon himself. Audubon offered contradictory accounts of his background. He told some people, perhaps in fun, that he was the lost son of the French monarchs Louis XVI and Marie-Antoinette. He also said that he had been born in New Orleans.

Neither account was true. John James Audubon was born in 1785 on the Audubon plantation in Saint-Domingue, now Haiti. His birth name was Jean Rabine; he was named after his mother, Jeanne, a slave who died when he was an infant. Audubon's father may have been a French naval officer, planter, merchant, or slave owner, or perhaps Captain Audubon himself. Three years later, the captain and his wife moved to France, where they adopted the boy and renamed him John James Audubon.

In 1803 Captain Audubon sent his son to Pennsylvania so that he would not be conscripted into Napoleon's army. While in the United States, Audubon discovered a passion for nature, especially for birds. He spent his days painting, hunting, and fishing. He later said that this was the happiest time of his life, even though he struggled financially and at one point was put in debtor's prison for a day.

As he grew older, Audubon never gave up his love of nature. He spent years traveling across the United States, observing, painting, collecting, and cataloguing birds. He wanted to create a record of every known bird species in the country. His great work, *Birds of America*, was published between 1827 and 1838. This volume, still consulted by professional and amateur ornithologists, described nearly 1,100 birds. Each entry included a lifelike watercolor or pastel painting of the bird and a detailed essay describing the bird's habitat, habits, and diet. The book appealed to artists and scientists alike.

After *Birds of America*, Audubon started a companion volume on mammals, *The Viviparous Quadrupeds of North America*. This work, which appeared between 1845 and 1848, was not the success that Audubon's previous work had been, but scientists still valued it. In 1851 John James Audubon died of a stroke at the age of 65.

gratitude—and a nickname, "Papa Doc"—from the poor Haitian villagers whom he had treated for a contagious and disfiguring disease called yaws, which afflicted up to three-fourths of the population.

Shortly after his inauguration, Duvalier discovered a plot to drive him from power. He quickly set about establishing a formidable security apparatus. From army units assigned to guard the presidential palace, he formed the Presidential Guard, a personal security force that also served as the unofficial police force of Port-au-Prince, the capital. Duvalier next created a special security force, the Volunteers for National Defense, or VSN. The members of the VSN—better known as the Tonton Macoutes—were drawn from the ranks of the poorest and least educated Haitians and were fiercely loyal to Duvalier. They intimidated and, if necessary, murdered the president's opponents with impunity.

The next pillar of Duvalier's power was voodoo, a religion based on African beliefs brought to Haiti by colonial-era

slaves. Devotees of voodoo worship the spirits of ancestors and believe that the spirits can intervene in everyday life. Duvalier was said to be a *houngan*, or priest in league with

At the time of his election as president in 1957, François Duvalier was a well-respected country doctor. His transformation into a ruthless dictator would not take long; by 1964 he had proclaimed himself Haiti's president for life.

the spirit world, and it was rumored that he had made a pilgrimage to the home of the spirits and brought them back to the presidential palace. Duvalier also invited *houngans* and *mambos* (priestesses) to the presidential palace. All of this was designed to convince Haitians that no mortal could ever remove the president from office.

By 1961 Papa Doc was in firm control of Haiti. He even changed the constitution so that he could be reelected indefinitely. In 1964 he proclaimed himself president for life. This last step ended democracy in Haiti and, along with his repressive rule, triggered the emigration of many educated professionals: health care workers, teachers, businesspeople, journalists, scientists, and skilled workers whose talents were desperately needed at home. In the early 1960s, Haitian immigrants entered Canada, the United States, and the African countries that had just become independent from France. Many Haitians, reluctant to move so far away, slipped across the border into the Dominican Republic.

After Fidel Castro set up a Communist government in Cuba, Duvalier curried favor with the United States by condemning the Castro regime. This anti-Communist stance earned Haiti millions of dollars in American foreign aid—much of which the president reportedly skimmed for his own use.

On April 21, 1971, François Duvalier died at the age of 65. During the 14 years he had ruled Haiti with an iron fist, at least 30,000 Haitians had been beaten, tortured, or killed; some simply vanished into the notorious Fort Dimanche Prison. Thousands of the country's most educated and skilled citizens had departed for other parts of the world.

Baby Doc Takes Over

Following the wishes of the late president, power passed to his only son, 19-year-old Jean-Claude Duvalier. Jean-Claude's youth and inexperience were considered advantages; people hoped that "Baby Doc," as he was called, would bring fresh ideas and break the cycle of dictatorship, poverty, and underdevelopment

The death of François Duvalier in April 1971 brought to power his son, Jean-Claude (fourth from right, holding white gloves in his left hand). Baby Doc, as the younger Duvalier was called, proved every bit as corrupt as his father.

that plagued Haiti.

These optimists were soon disappointed. "Jean Claude," a 1989 country report by the U.S. Library of Congress noted, "limited his interest in government to various fraudulent schemes and to outright misappropriation of funds." Baby Doc's extravagant 1980 wedding—a $3 million affair paid for with government funds—demonstrated just how oblivious the dictator was to the concerns of his impoverished subjects.

By the early 1980s conditions in Haiti were desperate. The economy was in a shambles. Tuberculosis and diarrhea were the leading causes of death, and the illiteracy rate exceeded 90 percent. To make matters worse, two new diseases, African swine flu (ASF) and acquired immune deficiency syndrome (AIDS), threatened the traditional ways of life.

ASF was a contagious but nonlethal disease that spread from wild to domesticated pigs. The disease frightened Haitian families, nearly all of whom had at least one lean, black Creole pig, which was kept on a tether or allowed to forage in the yard. The pig was not picky about what it ate, surviving on food scraps, garbage, and insects. The animal could be sold to pay for weddings, baptisms, funerals, or emergencies. In the fall, many families sold their pigs to pay school fees or purchase uniforms, books, and school supplies. Of course, the pig could also be eaten; pork was a major source of protein in the Haitian diet.

The United States and Canada pressured the Haitian authorities to slaughter all Creole pigs before ASF reached North America. In July 1981, Haiti signed an agreement allowing representatives of the Program for the Eradication of Porcine Swine Fever and the Development of Pig Raising (better known as PEPPADEP) to kill all Creole pigs.

In *Eyes of the Heart*, Jean-Bertrand Aristide, who would later become Haiti's president, describes what happened next:

> Two years later the new, better pigs came from Iowa. They were so much better that they required clean drinking water (unavailable to 80% of the Haitian population), imported feed (costing $90 a year when the per capita income was about $130), and special roofed pigpens. Haitian peasants quickly dubbed them "*prince à quatre pieds*" (four-footed princes). Adding insult to injury, the meat did not taste as good. Needless to say, the repopulation program was a complete failure. One observer of the process estimated that in monetary terms Haitian peasants lost $600 million. There was a 30% drop in enrollment in rural schools, there was a dramatic decline in the protein consumption in rural Haiti, a devastating decapitalization of the peasant economy and an incalculable negative impact on Haiti's soil and agricultural productivity. The Haitian peasantry has not recovered to this day.

The PEPPADEP program was a disaster. Without their pigs, many families could not send their children to school. School records showed that when PEPPADEP was in force, enrollments dropped by half. And since school was the one place where many children could receive one good meal a day, their absence meant that the schoolchildren were going hungry. The merchants who sold schoolbooks, uniforms, and supplies to students suffered because they had no customers.

AIDS struck next. A deadly disease caused by a virus that attacks the human immune system, AIDS appeared in Haiti shortly after the Duvalier government arranged for Club Mediterraneo to open a resort in Montrouis, where American and European tourists could enjoy the weather and the land-scape without slums to ruin the view. Because Haiti was one of the first countries where the previously unknown disease was identified, Haitians were incorrectly identified as a high-risk population or even labeled "AIDS carriers." The country's fledgling tourist industry was ruined.

Post-Duvalier Problems

By the mid-1980s the Duvalier regime was facing increasing pressure from a variety of sources. Haiti's decimated economy, years of political repression, and the excesses of the ruling family fueled anger among the country's impoverished majority. In the countryside, mobs attacked and murdered members of the hated Tonton Macoutes. In the cities, months of anti-government protests and riots turned the streets into battle-fields. And army officers, sensing perhaps that Baby Doc's days were numbered, refused to order their troops to fire on unarmed demonstrators, which further emboldened the opposition. The international community also joined in the chorus calling for Jean-Claude Duvalier to step down. The Reagan administration slashed U.S. aid to Haiti.

Finally, key members of the military, including Lieutenant General Henri Namphy, explained to Duvalier that he had to leave. Without the support of the military, the dictator could not hope to remain in power. On February 7, 1986, Jean-Claude Duvalier, his wife, and their children secretly boarded a U.S. Air Force C-141 cargo plane for France. Thus ended three decades of oppressive, corrupt rule by the Duvalier family.

But the departure of the Duvaliers did not solve Haiti's problems. Though a governing council consisting of military officers and civilians was set up, Namphy and the army held actual power, and they ruled harshly. The next four years brought a string of military takeovers, dictatorships, and a rigged election. The number of Haitians attempting to emigrate soared. Multinational companies that had planned to set up factories in Haiti withdrew because of the political turmoil.

Lieutenant General Henri Namphy (center) convinced Jean-Claude Duvalier to step aside in 1986. Namphy then ruled Haiti as the head of a military-dominated governing council until early 1988, when he briefly ceded power after presidential elections. After again seizing power in a June 1988 coup, Namphy was himself toppled by a coup three months later.

The tourist industry, still reeling from the AIDS scare, also stagnated because Haiti was not considered a safe vacation spot.

On March 29, 1987, a new constitution was ratified by 99.8 percent of Haitian voters. This constitution was Haiti's first to guarantee respect for human rights and to protect religious freedom, including the right to practice voodoo. Creole, the language spoken by more than 90 percent of Haiti's population, earned official status alongside French, the preferred tongue of the elite.

Yet in one respect the constitution limited political rights: supporters of the Duvaliers could not run for office or be appointed to any political position for 10 years. This clause would become a lightning rod for conflict between the new ruling parties and the Duvalierists.

Sunday, November 29, 1987, was to be Haiti's first free election in 30 years. Twenty-two candidates were vying for the presidency (two others had been murdered in the months before the election); also at stake were positions in the 27-seat

Mother Elizabeth

Elizabeth Clovis Lange, who would found the first religious order for blacks in the United States, was born in Saint-Domingue in 1784. In 1817 she and her mother moved to the United States, eventually settling in Baltimore, Maryland.

Baltimore was home to a large Haitian community of blacks, whites, and mulattos. French Roman Catholic priests were their spiritual leaders. Father Jacques Joubert had founded St. Mary's Seminary Chapel, the hub of the city's Haitian community. Like Haiti, the congregation was racially split, with the blacks meeting in the basement while the mulattos worshiped on the main floor.

Lange was appalled by the shortage of schools for Baltimore's black children, and she went to Father Joubert to request money for a school. She also wanted to become a nun. Father Joubert was receptive to both of Lange's suggestions. However, no Catholic religious order accepted black women, so Lange would have to start her own. While training for the religious life, Lange and a few of her friends began to raise money for the school.

Lange established the Oblate Sisters of Providence and took her final vows on July 2, 1829. Despite the encouragement of Father Joubert and Archbishop Whitfield of Baltimore, not everyone liked seeing black women in religious roles. One bishop wrote that Baltimore needed black housekeepers, not black nuns. In order to prevent such a bishop from dissolving her order, Lange sought and obtained official approval of the Oblate Sisters of Providence from the Vatican.

Mother Elizabeth was active in the educational community of Baltimore; several of her students became nuns and teachers in other parts of the country. By the time of her death in 1882, she had made education available for all black children in the Baltimore area.

Senate and 83-seat Chamber of Deputies.

After so many years without a political voice, Haitians were excited about the chance to vote. Lines at Haiti's 6,000 polling places were long, and as they waited to cast their ballots, many voters waved flags and sang songs in celebration of the day.

But not everyone wanted to see the elections go forward. Bands of armed men set fire to cars and trucks that were taking ballots to the polling places. In Port-au-Prince, prospective voters were attacked with clubs, rocks, and machetes. Some were even shot at. One reporter saw a line of voters sprayed with gunfire; when the gunmen had moved on, the survivors got up and returned to the line, determined to cast their vote at any cost. Dozens of people were killed, and many more wounded or beaten.

Almost immediately, Haitians and outside observers began speculating on who was responsible for the violence.

Haitians crowd into line to vote, November 29, 1987. Haiti's first free election in 30 years was marred by violence and voting irregularities, and Haiti's military rulers later invalidated the results.

Suspicion focused on Duvalier supporters, including members of the former Presidential Guard or Tonton Macoutes. The fact that the police and army had apparently done nothing to stop the violence indicated that Lieutenant General Namphy and Haiti's military rulers were involved as well—a suspicion that appeared confirmed when the government announced that the elections had to be invalidated, supposedly because of the chaos.

Early in 1988 military-sponsored elections that were widely boycotted, and generally considered fraudulent, brought a former director of Haiti's Foreign Ministry named Leslie Manigat to the presidency. But within a few months Namphy removed Manigat in a coup, dissolved the electoral council so that no new elections could be scheduled, and named himself president. Namphy, in turn, was later removed in a coup led by General Prosper Avril.

Though Avril appointed a civilian government, the military retained actual power.

A Step Forward, A Step Back

Pressure mounted, both within Haiti and abroad, for free and fair elections. In 1990 Haiti's leaders

An ordained Catholic priest and longtime activist for Haiti's poor, Jean-Bertrand Aristide (seen here addressing the United Nations General Assembly in 2003) won a landslide victory in presidential elections held in 1990. But Aristide was in office only seven months before being ousted by the military.

finally bowed to the pressure.

During the presidential campaign that year, one candidate stood out: Jean-Bertrand Aristide. An ordained Roman Catholic priest, Aristide had been an activist for Haiti's poor and homeless; a supporter of "liberation theology," the controversial set of principles emphasizing the moral responsibility of Christians to work for social and political justice; and a vocal critic of Jean-Claude Duvalier and the military regimes that succeeded Baby Doc. Aristide's political activities had gotten him expelled from the Salesians, the order of priests to which he belonged, and had led to an attempt on his life. But he remained enormously popular among Haiti's poor—and among the Haitian diaspora, which contributed most of the money for his presidential campaign.

Aristide's party, the National Front for Change and Democracy, was better known as Lavalas (a great tempest or flood). Its slogan appealed to poor Haitians' sense of solidarity: "Alone we are weak, together we are strong; all together we are Lavalas!"

On December 16, 1990—in presidential elections that international observers considered fair—Lavalas won a landslide at the polls. In the presidential race, two-thirds of all Haitian voters cast their ballots for Jean-Bertrand Aristide.

In his inaugural address, Aristide made a direct appeal to Haitians who lived abroad, urging them to assist their homeland. One of his first official actions was to create the Ministry for Haitians Living Abroad, which coordinated the activities of overseas Haitians with those at home. He was confident in the power of all Haitians to rebuild their country. Other elements of his program were a higher minimum wage, taxes on the wealthiest citizens, and protection of human rights. For the first time in years, allegations of human rights violations dropped, and money flowed into the government.

Haiti's experiment with democratic, civilian rule was short lived, however. In September 1991, after Aristide had been in office a mere seven months, the military seized control in a

coup. Aristide escaped to Venezuela, and from there made his way to New York.

General Raoul Cédras, the leader of the coup, clamped down hard on Aristide supporters. By all accounts, government-sponsored human rights violations, including torture, rape, and murder, were rampant. In addition to abuses committed by the army and police, a paramilitary group called the Front for the Advancement and Progress of Haiti, or FRAPH, terrorized opponents of the government with impunity.

International reaction to the overthrow of Aristide and the excesses of the Cédras regime was strong. The Organization of American States and the United Nations imposed economic sanctions. The United States and other nations withheld all or part of the foreign-aid money designated for Haiti; the United States also froze Haitian financial assets in U.S. banks and imposed a trade embargo. Human rights organizations joined Haitians throughout the diaspora in calling on all governments

Within months of the 1991 military takeover, thousands of Haitians had fled their country aboard a variety of seagoing vessels. Many of these boat people wanted asylum in the United States.

to step up the pressure on the Cédras regime.

For U.S. policymakers, concerns about the deteriorating situation in Haiti went beyond human rights issues. Large numbers of Haitians were taking to the high seas in small, often unsafe boats to escape the troubles in their homeland. Many were bound for U.S. shores. By the spring of 1992, the Coast Guard had intercepted some 38,000 Haitian boat people.

In July of 1993, in the face of mounting international pressure, the Cédras regime signed the Governor's Island Accord, a U.S.- and U.N.-mediated agreement for the restoration of democracy in Haiti. By the terms of the agreement, Haiti's military rulers were supposed to step down, and Jean-Bertrand Aristide was to return to the country as president, by October 30. As that deadline approached, however, government and FRAPH forces stepped up attacks on Aristide supporters, and Cédras ultimately refused to relinquish power.

By the following summer, President Bill Clinton had warned Haiti's military rulers to leave—or be removed by a U.S. invasion. Cédras vowed to fight.

In September the Clinton administration dispatched a delegation to Haiti to make one last effort to convince the regime that the

President Bill Clinton (right) with the high-level delegation he dispatched to Haiti to convince the country's military rulers to step down. From left: former president Jimmy Carter; Senator Sam Nunn; Colin Powell, former chairman of the Joint Chiefs of Staff.

United States was not bluffing. The delegation included former president Jimmy Carter; Colin Powell, the former chairman of the Joint Chiefs of Staff; and Senator Sam Nunn of Georgia, who was widely respected as an authority on military affairs. On September 18, with some U.S. invasion units already aboard their planes, Cédras agreed to step down and war was averted.

As part of "Operation Restore Democracy," about 20,000 U.S. troops landed in Haiti to ensure a peaceful transition to democracy. In October Cédras and his colleagues were allowed to go into exile in Panama, and a triumphant Aristide returned to Haiti to resume his presidency. U.S. and international sanctions were lifted, and—amid widespread optimism about the future—Haitians for the first time in years stopped trying to leave their country.

Promise and Disappointment

Local and national legislative elections in 1995 would begin to sour the outlook of a fair number of Haitians. Ten thousand men and women had campaigned for seats, and on Election Day in June, more than half of Haiti's 3.5 million eligible voters went to the polls. Because of the high turnout, some stations ran out of ballots, and in other places voters were still waiting in line when the polls closed. There were so many complaints that the government scheduled a makeup election for August. This did not please everyone—especially when the results of the August balloting showed Lavalas supporters winning most of the seats in the legislature and in local governments. Opposition parties refused to believe that the elections had been fair.

More controversy arose the following year, when Aristide's presidential term was set to expire. Although the 1987 Haitian constitution barred presidents from serving consecutive terms, Aristide argued that he should be permitted to run for reelection because the coup had cut his term short by three years. When reminded of his earlier promises to respect the constitution, Aristide abandoned his plan for another term and threw his support behind René Préval, whom he described as his "twin brother."

Beyond a brief stint as prime minister in 1991, Préval had little political experience. He did not have a college degree, and for most of his life he had worked in a bakery. Observers speculated that Aristide wanted Préval to be a caretaker president until 2000, when Aristide would be eligible to run for another five-year term. In any event, Préval won the election in a landslide that most analysts attributed more to Aristide's influence than to Préval's gifts as a campaigner.

Almost from the beginning, the new president's administration was paralyzed by conflict with lawmakers. At one point Préval even shut down the legislature. Largely because of these disputes, little tangible progress was made during his term.

In 2000, as expected, Aristide ran for president again. But many Haitians were profoundly disillusioned by this second campaign. Critics suggest that, in his zeal to prove that he had the mandate of the Haitian people, Aristide wanted not simply to win the election, but to win it in a landslide. And to guarantee that outcome, the critics say, the man once revered as the "people's hero" used the same strong-arm tactics that had once been the specialty of Haiti's military dictators. Fifteen candidates who opposed the Lavalas platform were assassinated; many journalists and ordinary citizens were murdered as well. An Aristide aide claimed that the violence was being carried out by a small minority who did not represent the principles of the party. Aristide's silence on the matter, however, was eloquent.

In protest, opposition parties boycotted the election, and voter turnout was a meager 10 percent. Aristide claimed his landslide victory—official tallies gave him more than 90 percent of the votes cast—but reports of voting irregularities and fraud were widespread. Many neutral observers abroad believed that Aristide was beginning to act like the dictators he had been famous for denouncing.

"Aristide is not a man who knows how to compromise," said

Aristide supporters at a 2003 demonstration in Port-au-Prince. The five fingers extended signifies the determination to see Aristide serve the full five years of his presidential term, despite persistent calls by opponents that he step down.

Evans Paul, a former supporter. "He does not like to be questioned. He does not accept advice. There is no other way of seeing things than his way. . . . He already is a dictator."

The ugliness that surrounded Aristide's second presidential campaign continued during his second term in office. In December 2001, commandos believed to have ties to Haiti's armed forces stormed the presidential palace in an apparent coup attempt but were beaten back by police and army units loyal to the president after a fierce firefight. In the weeks and months that followed, armed gangs attacked and murdered dozens of journalists, Aristide critics, and opposition politicians. Many Haitians suspected that these gangs operated with the blessing of—and were perhaps even directed by—Lavalas officials. Farmers, university students, members of the clergy, and others who had previously supported Aristide took to the streets in angry protests denouncing the president. Often the demonstrators clashed with police and Aristide supporters. Haiti's already weak economy reeled under the weight of worker strikes. Although some observers wondered whether Haiti might be better off if Aristide resigned, the president vowed to serve until his term expired in early 2006.

3 HAITIAN IMMIGRATION TO NORTH AMERICA

North America in recent decades has seen an upsurge in Haitian immigration. Official U.S. immigration statistics, for example, record fewer than 4,500 Haitian immigrants in the period 1951–1960, but about 34,500 the following decade; by 1991–2000 the figure topped 179,600. In addition to those admitted as legal immigrants, tens of thousands of Haitians have, at various times, attempted to gain admission to the United States as refugees, and about 76,000 lived within U.S. borders as undocumented migrants as of 2000, according to U.S. government estimates.

To a certain extent the patterns of Haitian migration to North America can be linked to political and economic conditions in Haiti. When, for example, government oppression has been particularly severe, large numbers of Haitians have sought to leave. But immigration is also affected by laws and policies in the destination countries. To place immigration from Haiti in context, it is useful to look briefly at the history of U.S. and Canadian immigration.

A Brief History of U.S. Immigration to 1965

Immigration to the United States has been characterized by openness punctuated by periods of restriction. During the 17th, 18th, and 19th centuries, immigration was essentially open without restriction, and, at times, immigrants were even

◀Nearly 470 Haitian migrants were crowded aboard this old freighter, which was interdicted by the U.S. Coast Guard in October 1988. During the 1980s and 1990s, Haiti's political problems spurred tens of thousands of citizens to risk their lives attempting a sea passage to Florida.

Immigrants from certain countries have not always been welcomed into the United States. This cartoon, published in 1881 in the San Francisco–based magazine the *Wasp*, attributes a host of social ills, including immorality, disease, filth, and the ruin of "white labor," to Chinese immigrants. The following year, Congress passed the Chinese Exclusion Act of 1882, which essentially cut off immigration from China.

recruited to come to America. Between 1783 and 1820, approximately 250,000 immigrants arrived at U.S. shores. Between 1841 and 1860, more than 4 million immigrants came; most were from England, Ireland, and Germany.

Historically, race and ethnicity have played a role in legislation to restrict immigration. The Chinese Exclusion Act of 1882, which was not repealed until 1943, specifically prevented Chinese people from becoming U.S. citizens and did not allow Chinese laborers to immigrate for the next decade. An agreement with Japan in the early 1900s prevented most Japanese immigration to the United States.

Until the 1920s, no numerical restrictions on immigration existed in the United States, although health restrictions applied. The only other significant restrictions came in 1917, when passing a literacy test became a requirement for immigrants. Presidents Cleveland, Taft, and Wilson had vetoed similar measures earlier. In addition, in 1917 a prohibition was added to the law against the immigration of people from Asia (defined as the Asiatic barred zone). While a few of these prohibitions were lifted during World War II, they were not

From Slavery to Philanthropy

At the intersection of Barclay Street and Church Street in New York City is Pierre Toussaint Square, named for the philanthropist who may become not only the first Haitian-born saint, but also the first North American black saint.

Pierre Toussaint was born between 1756 and 1766 on the Bérard family plantation. Though he was a slave, his master saw that the boy learned to read and write, and one biographer described the young Pierre as "the pet of the plantation." In 1793 the Haitian slave rebellion forced the Bérards to flee to New York City, with Pierre and his younger sister Rosalie. Mr. Bérard returned to Haiti to recover some of his property, but died there of pleurisy.

In New York, Mrs. Bérard had Toussaint trained as a hairdresser. For years, until she remarried, Toussaint's wages sustained the household. On her deathbed in 1807, she freed him. Still, Toussaint worked 16 hours a day, first to purchase the freedom of his sister, and then to purchase the freedom of Juliette, the woman that he married in 1811.

Throughout his life, Toussaint kept only enough money to support his wife and his niece Euphémie, the daughter of Toussaint's late sister. The rest went to charities or to friends. Toussaint gave money to the children of refugees from Haiti and France, he paid for the vocational training of black boys, and he was one of the first to donate to the Sisters of Charity, an order of nuns who wanted to open an orphanage. Although he made regular contributions to the construction of Saint Patrick's Cathedral, as a black man he was forbidden to attend Mass there. During the yellow fever epidemic, Toussaint and his wife nursed the sickest victims in their own home.

Toussaint's integrity, generosity, and knowledge of Catholic theology were so well known that his friends called him "Saint Pierre." He died in 1853.

In 1968 the Roman Catholic Church began the first steps toward canonizing Toussaint (that is, officially declaring him a saint). In 1990 his remains were moved to a crypt under St. Patrick's Cathedral, a New York City landmark his generosity helped build.

repealed until 1952, and even then Asians were only allowed in under very small annual quotas.

During World War I, the federal government required that all travelers to the United States obtain a visa at a U.S. consulate or diplomatic post abroad. As former State Department consular affairs officer C. D. Scully points out, by making that requirement permanent Congress, by 1924, established the framework of temporary, or non-immigrant visas (for study, work, or travel), and immigrant visas (for permanent residence). That framework remains in place today.

After World War I, cultural intolerance and bizarre racial theories led to new immigration restrictions. The House Judiciary Committee employed a eugenics consultant, Dr. Harry N. Laughlin, who asserted that certain races were inferior. Another leader of the eugenics movement, Madison Grant, argued that Jews, Italians, and others were inferior because of their supposedly different skull size.

The Immigration Act of 1924, preceded by the Temporary Quota Act of 1921, set new numerical limits on immigration based on "national origin." Taking effect in 1929, the 1924 act set annual quotas on immigrants that were specifically designed to keep out southern Europeans, such as Italians and Greeks. Generally no more than 100 people of the proscribed nationalities were permitted to immigrate.

While the new law was rigid, the U.S. Department of State's restrictive interpretation directed consular officers overseas to be even stricter in their application of the "public charge" provision. (A public charge is someone unable to support himself or his family.) According to author Laura Fermi, "In response to the new cry for restriction at the beginning of the [Great Depression] . . . the consuls were to interpret very strictly the clause prohibiting admission of aliens 'likely to become public charges; and to deny the visa to an applicant who in their opinion might become a public charge at any time.'"

In the early 1900s, more than one million immigrants a year came to the United States. In 1930—the first year of the national-origin quotas—approximately 241,700 immigrants were admitted. But under the State Department's strict interpretations, only 23,068 immigrants entered during 1933, the smallest total since 1831. Later these restrictions prevented many Jews in Germany and elsewhere in Europe from escaping what would become the Holocaust. At the height of the Holocaust in 1943, the United States admitted fewer than 6,000 refugees.

The Displaced Persons Act of 1948, the nation's first refugee law, allowed many refugees from World War II to settle in the United States. The law put into place policy changes that had already seen immigration rise from 38,119 in 1945 to 108,721 in 1946 (and later to 249,187 in 1950). One-third of those admitted between 1948 and 1951 were Poles, with ethnic Germans forming the second-largest group.

The 1952 Immigration and Nationality Act is best known for its restrictions against those who supported communism or anarchy. However, the bill's other provisions were quite restrictive and were passed over the veto of President Truman. The 1952 act retained the national-origin quota system for the Eastern Hemisphere. The Western Hemisphere continued to operate without a quota and relied on other qualitative factors to limit immigration. Moreover, during that time, the Mexican bracero program, from 1942 to 1964, allowed millions of Mexican agricultural laborers to work temporarily in the United States.

The 1952 act set aside half of each national quota to be divided among three preference categories for relatives of U.S. citizens and permanent residents. The other half went to aliens with high education or exceptional abilities. These quotas applied only to those from the Eastern Hemisphere.

An End to the National-Origin Quotas

The Immigration and Nationality Act of 1965 became a landmark in immigration legislation by specifically striking the racially based national-origin quotas. It removed the barriers to

Asian immigration, which later led to opportunities to immigrate for many Filipinos, Chinese, Koreans, and others. The Western Hemisphere was designated a ceiling of 120,000 immigrants but without a preference system or per country limits. Modifications made in 1978 ultimately combined the Western and Eastern Hemispheres into one preference system and one ceiling of 290,000.

The 1965 act built on the existing system—without the national-origin quotas—and gave somewhat more priority to family relationships. It did not completely overturn the existing system but rather carried forward essentially intact the family immigration categories from the 1959 amendments to the Immigration and Nationality Act. Even though the text of the law prior to 1965 indicated that half of the immigration slots were reserved for skilled employment immigration, in practice, Immigration and Naturalization Service (INS) statistics show

Upon signing into law the Immigration Act of 1965, President Lyndon B. Johnson declared that the national-origin quota system would "never again shadow the gate to the American nation with the twin barriers of prejudice and privilege."

that 86 percent of the visas issued between 1952 and 1965 went for family immigration.

A number of significant pieces of legislation since 1980 have shaped the current U.S. immigration system. First, the Refugee Act of 1980 removed refugees from the annual world limit and established that the president would set the number of refugees who could be admitted each year after consultations with Congress.

Second, the 1986 Immigration Reform and Control Act (IRCA) introduced sanctions against employers who "knowingly" hired undocumented immigrants (those in the country illegally). It also provided amnesty for many undocumented immigrants.

Third, the Immigration Act of 1990 increased legal immigration by 40 percent. In particular, the act significantly increased the number of employment-based immigrants (to 140,000) while also boosting family immigration.

Fourth, the 1996 Illegal Immigration Reform and Immigrant Responsibility Act (IIRAIRA) significantly tightened rules that permitted undocumented immigrants to convert to legal status and made other changes that tightened immigration law in areas such as political asylum and deportation.

Fifth, in response to the September 11, 2001, terrorist attacks, the USA PATRIOT Act and the Enhanced Border Security and Visa Entry Reform Act tightened rules on the granting of visas to individuals from certain countries and enhanced the federal government's monitoring and detention authority over foreign nationals in the United States.

New U.S. Immigration Agencies

In a dramatic reorganization of the federal government, the Homeland Security Act of 2002 abolished the Immigration and Naturalization Service and transferred its immigration service and enforcement functions from the Department of Justice into the new Department of Homeland Security. The Customs Service, the Coast Guard, and parts of other agencies were also transferred into the new department.

The Department of Homeland Security, with regard to immigration, is organized as follows: The Bureau of Customs and Border Protection (BCBP) contains Customs and Immigration inspectors, who check the documents of travelers to the United States at air, sea, and land ports of entry; and Border Patrol agents, the uniformed agents who seek to prevent unlawful entry along the southern and northern border. The new Bureau of Immigration and Customs Enforcement (BICE) employs investigators, who attempt to find undocumented immigrants inside the United States, and Detention and Removal officers, who detain and seek to deport such individuals. U.S. Citizenship and Immigration Services (USCIS)—formerly the Bureau of Citizenship and Immigration Services (BCIS)—is where people

Attorney General John Ashcroft defends the USA PATRIOT Act in a speech before law enforcement personnel in Detroit, August 21, 2003. The controversial act, which Ashcroft maintained was necessary to combat the threat of terrorism, gave the government additional powers to monitor and detain foreign nationals in the United States.

go, or correspond with, to become U.S. citizens or obtain permission to work or extend their stay in the United States.

Following the terrorist attacks of September 11, 2001, the Department of Justice adopted several measures that did not require new legislation to be passed by Congress. Some of these measures created controversy and raised concerns about civil liberties. For example, FBI and INS agents detained for months more than 1,000 foreign nationals of Middle Eastern descent and refused to release the names of the individuals. It is alleged that the Department of Justice adopted tactics that discouraged the detainees from obtaining legal assistance. The Department of Justice also began requiring foreign nationals from primarily Muslim nations to be fingerprinted and questioned by immigration officers upon entry or if they have been living in the United States. Those involved in the September 11 attacks were not immigrants—people who become permanent residents with a right to stay in the United States—but holders of temporary visas, primarily visitor or tourist visas.

Recent Developments

Today, the annual rate of legal immigration is lower than that at earlier periods in U.S. history. For example, from 1901 to 1910 approximately 10.4 immigrants per 1,000 U.S. residents came to the United States. Today, the annual rate is about 3.5 immigrants per 1,000 U.S. residents. While the percentage of foreign-born people in the U.S. population has risen above 11 percent, it remains lower than the 13 percent or higher that prevailed in the country from 1860 to 1930. Still, as has been the case previously in U.S. history, some people argue that even legal immigration should be lowered. These people maintain that immigrants take jobs native-born Americans could fill and that U.S. population growth, to which immigration contributes, harms the environment.

Most immigrants (800,000 to one million annually) enter the United States legally. But over the years the undocumented (illegal) portion of the population has increased to about 2.8 per-

The first page of the form foreign citizens must fill out to apply for an immigrant visa to the United States.

cent of the U.S. population—approximately 8 million people in all.

Today, the legal immigration system in the United States contains many rules, permitting only individuals who fit into certain categories to immigrate—and in many cases only after waiting anywhere from 1 to 10 years or more, depending on the demand in that category. The system, representing a compromise among family, employment, and human rights concerns, has the following elements:

A U.S. citizen may sponsor for immigration a spouse, parent, sibling, or minor or adult child.

A lawful permanent resident (green card holder) may sponsor only a spouse or child.

A foreign national may immigrate if he or she gains an employer sponsor.

An individual who can show that he or she has a "well-founded fear of persecution" may come to the country as a refugee—or be allowed to stay as an asylee (someone who receives asylum).

Beyond these categories, essentially the only other way to immigrate is to apply for and receive one of the "diversity" visas, 50,000 of which are granted annually by lottery to those from "underrepresented" countries.

In 1996 changes to the law prohibited nearly all incoming immigrants from being eligible for federal public benefits, such as welfare, during their first five years in the country. Refugees were mostly excluded from these changes. In addition, families who sponsor relatives must sign an affidavit of support showing they can financially take care of an immigrant who falls on hard times.

A Short History of Canadian Immigration

In the 1800s, immigration into Canada was largely unrestricted. Farmers and artisans from England and Ireland made up a significant portion of 19th-century immigrants. England's Parliament passed laws that facilitated and encouraged the voyage to North America, particularly for the poor.

After the United States barred Chinese railroad workers from settling in the country, Canada encouraged the immigration of Chinese laborers to assist in the building of Canadian railways. Responding to the racial views of the time, however, the Canadian Parliament began charging a "head tax" for Chinese and South Asian (Indian) immigrants in 1885. The fee of $50—later raised to $500—was well beyond the means of laborers making one or two dollars a day. Later, the government sought additional ways to prohibit Asians from entering the country. For example, it decided to require a "continuous journey," meaning that immigrants to Canada had to travel from their country on a boat that made an uninterrupted passage. For immigrants or asylum seekers from Asia, this was nearly impossible.

As the 20th century progressed, concerns about race led to further restrictions on immigration to Canada. These restrictions particularly hurt Jewish and other refugees seeking to flee persecution in Europe. Government statistics indicate that Canada accepted no more than 5,000 Jewish refugees before and during the Holocaust.

After World War II, Canada, like the United States, began accepting thousands of Europeans displaced by the war. Canada's laws were modified to permit the admission of these war refugees, as well as Hungarians fleeing Communist authorities after the crushing of the 1956 Hungarian Revolution.

The Immigration Act of 1952 in Canada allowed for a "tap on, tap off" approach to immigration, granting administrative authorities the power to allow more immigrants into the country in good economic times, and fewer in times of recession. The shortcoming of such an approach is that there is little evidence immigrants harm a national economy and much evidence they contribute to economic growth, particularly in the growth of the labor force.

In 1966 the government of Prime Minister Lester Pearson introduced a policy statement stressing how immigrants were key to Canada's economic growth. With Canada's relatively small population base, it became clear that in the absence of newcomers, the country would not be able to grow. The policy was introduced four years after Parliament enacted important legislation that eliminated Canada's own version of racially based national-origin quotas.

In 1967 a new law established a points system that awarded entry to potential immigrants using criteria based primarily on an individual's age, language ability, skills, education, family relationships, and job prospects. The total points needed for entry of an immigrant is set by the Minister of Citizenship and Immigration Canada. The new law also established a category for humanitarian (refugee) entry.

The 1976 Immigration Act refined and expanded the possibility for entry under the points system, particularly for those seeking to sponsor family members. The act also expanded refugee and asylum law to comport with Canada's international obligations. The law established five basic categories for immigration into Canada: 1) family; 2) humanitarian; 3) independents (including skilled workers), who immigrate to Canada

Lester Pearson, who served as Canada's prime minister between 1963 and 1968, believed that immigrants were crucial to his country's long-term economic prospects.

on their own; 4) assisted relatives; and 5) business immigrants (including investors, entrepreneurs, and the self-employed).

The new Immigration and Refugee Protection Act, which took effect June 28, 2002, made a series of modifications to existing Canadian immigration law. The act, and the regulations that followed, toughened rules on those seeking asylum and the process for removing people unlawfully in Canada.

The law modified the points system, adding greater flexibility for skilled immigrants and temporary workers to become permanent residents, and evaluating skilled workers on the weight of their transferable skills as well as those of their specific occupation. The legislation also made it easier for employers to have a labor shortage declared in an industry or sector, which would facilitate the entry of foreign workers in that industry or sector.

On family immigration, the act permitted parents to sponsor dependent children up to the age of 22 (previously 19 was the maximum age at which a child could be sponsored for immigration). The act also allowed partners in common-law arrangements, including same-sex partners, to be considered as family members for the purpose of immigration sponsorship.

Along with these liberalizing measures, the act also included provisions to address perceived gaps in immigration-law enforcement.

Haitians in the Dominican Republic

Haitian emigration is as old as the country of Haiti itself. But the size of the Haitian community living abroad remained relatively small until the last four decades of the 20th century. Since 1957, when François Duvalier came to power, conservative estimates put the number of Haitians who have left their homeland at more than 1 million.

Haitians have settled in a variety of countries, including African nations such as Congo and Guinea; France; Canada; the Bahamas; and Cuba (although Fidel Castro stopped Haitian workers from immigrating to the island after taking power in 1959). But the two countries that have attracted the largest number of Haitian immigrants are the Dominican

Dominican dictator Rafael Trujillo (center) ordered a massacre of Haitians living within his country in October 1937. The incident, during which some 30,000 people were killed, continues to strain relations between Haitians and Dominicans. Still, about a million Haitians live in the Dominican Republic, primarily for economic reasons.

Republic and the United States.

It's not surprising that the Dominican Republic would be a popular destination for Haitians. The two countries share the island of Hispaniola, and crossing the border is easy. Poor Haitians are attracted to their eastern neighbor by the prospect of employment there; the Dominican Republic has a more developed economy and a higher standard of living. Although many Haitians have taken up long-term residence in the Dominican Republic, many others find temporary or seasonal employment and move back and forth between the two countries. An estimated quarter of a million Haitians live legally in the Dominican Republic; the number of undocumented Haitians may be higher.

Despite the large number of Haitians who choose to settle in the Dominican Republic, relations with the Dominican people are often strained. Part of this is based in historical grievances: Haiti invaded and ruled its neighbor for 20 years during the 19th century; the Dominican dictator Rafael Leonidas Trujillo ordered a massacre of Haitians in October 1937, and over the course of several weeks 30,000 Haitians living in the northwestern Dominican Republic were hacked to death by machete-wielding soldiers. Race also plays a role: the generally fairer-skinned Dominicans tend to emphasize their Hispanic heritage, whereas 95 percent of Haitians are black. Economics, too, is a source of friction. While the Dominican Republic is well off in comparison with Haiti, one in four Dominicans lives below the poverty line, and unemployment in the early years of the 21st century hovered near 15 percent. Many Dominicans accuse Haitians of stealing "their" jobs. Many Haitians, on the other hand, complain that Dominican employers exploit them as a source of cheap labor.

Haitian Migration to the United States

Haitian immigration to the United States remained negligible until the latter half of the 20th century; in fact, 1932 is the first year Haitians were counted separately in immigration statistics, and fewer than 200 arrived during the remainder of the decade. The period 1941–1950 saw fewer than 1,000 Haitian immigrants admitted into the United States; during the next decade, 4,442 Haitians arrived—only 445 per year.

The first large-scale immigration to the United States from Haiti took place during the 1960s. By then François Duvalier, elected president in 1957, had consolidated his power and ruled Haiti as a dictator. Freedom of speech was nonexistent. Newspapers and radio stations were run by the state, offering only the official point of view. Individuals who dared to criti-

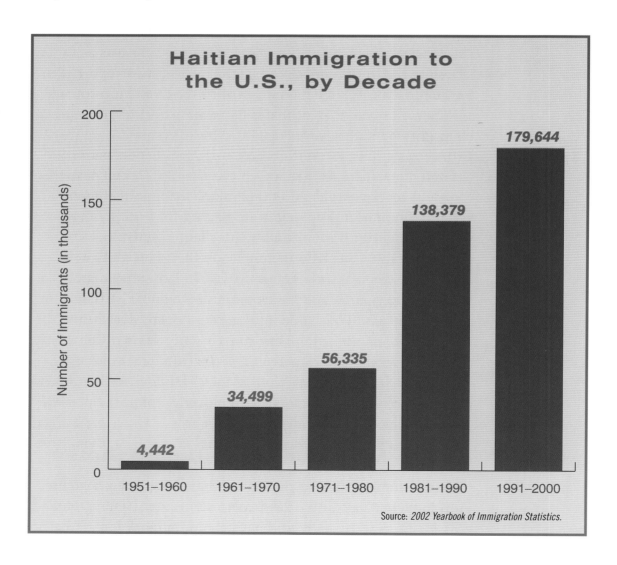

Haitian Immigration to the U.S., by Decade

Source: *2002 Yearbook of Immigration Statistics.*

cize Duvalier's regime were dealt with ruthlessly—arrested, tortured, and, in many cases, murdered by the Presidential Guard or the Tonton Macoutes. Between 1961 and 1970, a total of 34,499 Haitians immigrated to the United States, according to INS statistics. Many were among Haiti's best-educated citizens, and those a country struggling economically could least afford to lose: doctors, teachers, skilled workers.

In addition to those fortunate enough to obtain immigration visas during the 14-year dictatorship of Papa Doc, many other Haitians sought to leave their homeland without permission. This could be a very dangerous choice. Duvalier viewed the high rates of emigration from his country as a personal insult, stating that any Haitian who chose to live abroad was a traitor. Departure points for undocumented Haitians were reportedly kept under surveillance by the Tonton Macoutes, who sometimes attacked the would-be migrants when they gathered to begin their secret passage overseas.

François Duvalier's death in 1971 brought a short period of optimism for Haitians. But those who had hoped that Jean-Claude Duvalier would be a more enlightened ruler than his father were soon disappointed—and, after a brief decline in the number of Haitians leaving their homeland, legal and unauthorized emigration increased substantially. Between 1971 and 1980, the United States admitted 56,335 Haitian immigrants.

In 1972, U.S. officials observed the start of a trend that before long would become a source of great consternation. Haitians fleeing the regime began arriving in Florida aboard a variety of seagoing vessels, including (particularly in later years) homemade craft. By 1981 the INS had counted 55,000 of these "boat people." Depending on conditions at sea and the type of vessel, their journey might have taken a week or longer; and an unknown number never reached U.S. shores, dying en route from drowning, dehydration, or exposure.

Those boat people who were fortunate enough to arrive in Florida typically requested asylum in the United States upon apprehension by immigration authorities. According to U.S.

law, to be considered for asylum a person must be "unable or unwilling to return to his or her country of nationality because of persecution or a well-founded fear of persecution." Essentially asylum seekers claim that being sent back to their home country would expose them to danger. But a generally oppressive political climate is insufficient to prevail in an asylum claim; those who seek asylum in the United States must demonstrate an *individualized* danger—they must show that they personally are at risk. Under this requirement, Haitians had difficulty obtaining asylum in the United States—many critics claimed unjustly so. Whereas people fleeing Communist countries (for example, Cuba) were typically granted asylum, INS asylum examiners tended to view Haitians as fleeing economic hardship, not individual political oppression.

In any case, to stem the wave of unauthorized Haitian migrants, the United States in 1981 signed an interdiction agreement with Haiti. The agreement gave the United States Coast Guard the right to intercept and board boats on the high seas that were transporting Haitians. Usually individual Haitians had to tell the Coast Guard (or INS) that they feared persecution or they were not given a chance to pursue an asylum claim. According to the Congressional Research Service, 22,940 Haitians were intercepted at sea between 1981 and 1990, and only 11 were allowed to apply for asylum by the U.S. government; the rest were returned to Haiti.

Haitians who had arrived during the time of the Mariel boat lift in 1980 fared a bit better. The Mariel boat lift was a massive migration of Cubans to Miami. With the acquiescence of Cuba's dictator, Fidel Castro, more than 125,000 Cubans left the island over a seven-month period. During the same period, more than 25,000 Haitians arrived in South Florida. Although many of these Haitians could not pass the standard of being persecuted on an individual basis, the 1986 Immigration Reform and Control Act labeled those arriving during this time as Cuban-Haitian entrants (though it was primarily Haitians who were affected) and gave them an opportunity to become green card holders, or lawful permanent residents.

The year 1986 also saw the ouster of Jean-Claude Duvalier. But the governments led by the generals Henri Namphy and Prosper Avril proved equally repressive, and legal and unauthorized migration continued at high levels. INS statistics show that 138,379 Haitian immigrants were admitted into the United States during the period 1981–1990.

Although 1991 began with the promise of better times in Haiti, the military coup of September 30 ousted President Aristide and ended the country's brief experiment with democratic rule. Hundreds of Haitians were killed in the days following the military takeover, and over the next few months, tens of thousands attempted to flee the country.

In November the U.S. Coast Guard interdicted more than 400 Haitian refugees in boats. With the help of the United Nations High Commissioner for Refugees (UNHCR), Belize, Honduras, and other countries in the region agreed to provide a temporary haven for some of the Haitians. But that arrangement quickly

By late 1991 Haitians interdicted at sea were being taken to the U.S. naval base at Guantánamo Bay, Cuba, where they lived in tent cities pending a hearing to determine whether they had legitimate asylum claims.

proved insufficient to deal with the steadily increasing numbers of Haitian boat people the Coast Guard was picking up. By the end of 1991 the United States was taking rescued boat people to the U.S. naval base in Guantánamo Bay, Cuba. There the Haitians lived in tent cities pending a hearing of their asylum claims.

By the spring of 1992 the Coast Guard had intercepted 38,000 Haitian refugees since Aristide was forced from power. More than 10,400 of those brought to Guantánamo were paroled into the United States after having been screened at the naval base and found to have a credible fear of persecution, meaning they had some chance of gaining asylum in a full-fledged interview with the INS.

However, in May 1992 President George Bush signed an executive order directing that Haitians intercepted at sea be immediately returned to Haiti; no interviews would be conducted to determine whether individuals might be at risk of persecution. This decision was controversial, and human rights organizations such as Amnesty International viewed it as a violation of international law. In July 1992, the Second Circuit Court of Appeals ruled against the Bush administration's policy of not screening individual Haitians for refugee status, although the Supreme Court did not uphold the appeals court ruling.

Also during the Bush administration, in-country processing for potential Haitian refugees began. In other words, claims for refugee status were evaluated while the Haitians remained in Haiti.

In-country processing continued during the administration of Bush's successor, Bill Clinton. In fact, the Clinton administration adopted much the same approach to the Haitian refugee problem as had the Bush administration. Even though Clinton had, as a presidential candidate, criticized Bush's policy of forcibly returning Haitians, he essentially continued that policy after taking office in 1993. The Clinton administration also expanded on the Bush administration's efforts with UNHCR by placing Haitians who expressed a fear of persecution in safe havens in third countries, not allowing them into the United States.

Legal immigration from Haiti peaked in 1991, the year President Aristide was ousted by the military. The United States admitted 47,527 Haitian immigrants that year, up from 20,324 in 1990. In the years after the coup, immigration fell sharply, to 11,002, and it remained low during the next two years (10,094 in 1993, and 13,333 in 1994). The years following the restoration of civilian rule—under the presidencies of Aristide, René Préval, and Aristide again—have seen generally increasing levels of Haitian immigration to the United States, as Haiti has continued to struggle with economic and political problems. Overall, 179,644 Haitian immigrants came to the United States in the period 1991–2000, and immigration remained relatively high in 2001 and 2002, standing at 27,120 and 20,268, respectively.

Meanwhile, significant numbers of Haitian asylum-seekers continued to leave their country aboard boats. In 2001 about 7,800 Haitians applied for asylum in the United States, Canada, and France. More than 5,000 of these applicants wanted to live in the United States. Twenty-four percent of the applications were approved, representing a slight increase over previous years.

At the end of 2001, the administration of President George W. Bush initiated a controversial policy: all Haitians who made it to U.S. soil via boat were to be detained. Attorney General John Ashcroft argued that the policy was necessary to prevent a "mass migration." And, in the spring of 2003, Ashcroft invoked "national security" to justify the continuing detention of the Haitians. This policy meant that rather than being let out on bond while their asylum claims before immigration judges were being decided, Haitian men and women would remain locked up for nine months or more in prison, albeit separated from criminals.

4 MAKING A NEW LIFE

More than a million people have left Haiti since 1957, the first year of the Duvalier era. Their descendants may never have lived in Haiti, but they remain part of it through emotional, economic, and, most significantly, family ties.

The Importance of Family

Family is extremely important to Haitians, whose idea of family includes not only parents and children but also grandparents, aunts, uncles, and cousins. Each Haitian is born into an extended community of blood, marriage, and informal adoption.

For Haitians, obligation to family members is a central value. And this obligation does not lessen with distance—if anything, it increases. Haitian families expect those living abroad to contribute to those who remain in Haiti. And each year, Haitians in the diaspora send hundreds of millions of dollars home—to their parents, their siblings, their children, and needy members of their extended family. During particularly difficult times, these cash remittances have amounted to more than the total of foreign aid that Haiti receives from other governments. Haitians living abroad also send clothing, toiletries, household items, food, books, medicines, and other goods that relatives have requested. In a desperately poor country like Haiti, remittances often make the difference

◀Haitians place tremendous importance on family. Those living and working abroad are expected to send home money—as well as clothes, household items, medicines, and other supplies—to support their relatives in Haiti.

between getting by and struggling to survive.

Because a greater number of family members living abroad means more remittances flowing into the sponsoring household, Haitians tend to view emigration in fairly positive terms. It represents not so much the loss of a family member as a change in his or her role. Rather than helping to support the family at home, the emigrant is helping to support it from abroad.

Those living outside Haiti play another important role besides sending home remittances: they take care of family members newly arrived in the country, who are called "just-comes." Haitian migration patterns may appear random to outsiders, but they are actually quite systematic. Families arrange for the sequential migration of members, so that each new arrival will have a network of family and friends to help him or her settle in. Because extended Haitian families may include hundreds of people, it is rare to find Haitian Americans who do not still have relatives in Haiti.

Upon arrival the just-come will typically stay with relatives until he or she can get established in the new country and find

For many new Haitian immigrants, or just-comes, the key to finding a job is the network of family members and friends who are already established in the community.

another place to live. It is not unusual for a just-come to spend months or even years living with family members, sometimes by moving from one relative's home to another's. Haitian households, whether in Haiti or in the diaspora, are known for their unconditional hospitality. Even families that are struggling always seem able to find a bed and a place at the table for a newcomer.

Although most Haitians accept their many family obligations, some immigrants express frustration at the unrealistic ideas their relatives back home have about what life outside Haiti is like. Family members in Haiti frequently assume that their kin in wealthy countries such as the United States and Canada live in luxury and can afford to send large remittances. But the reality is often much different. The cost of living in North America is much higher than it is in Haiti, and many Haitian immigrants must work several jobs just to make ends meet.

Finding Work

If finding employment is the reason a large proportion of Haitian emigrants leave their homeland, many Haitians arrive in the United States and Canada with few job skills and comparatively little education—which puts them at a disadvantage in the North American labor market. For these just-comes particularly, the social network formed by family members and friends is vital in securing a good economic future.

Established immigrants, in addition to providing just-comes with food and a place to live, frequently alert them to job opportunities. In addition, the members of a Haitian social network—newcomers as well as those who have lived abroad for years—often pool resources, enabling them to take advantage of job opportunities. For example, one woman in a social network might provide child care while others are at work, or a number of people might share transportation costs.

Many Haitians in North America, particularly during the first years after their arrival, work in low-wage, low-skill occupations—for example, as farm or factory laborers, janitors, or restaurant or hotel workers. And a substantial number make ends meet by working several jobs. A Haitian woman might clean houses some days, take care of children at night, and make clothes when she has the time. A man might have a part-time job as a restaurant dishwasher, then repair electronic equipment or automobiles for people in the neighborhood and drive a gypsy cab on weekends.

But other Haitians have also established their own thriving businesses. "The Haitians are very entrepreneurial people and

Most Haitian immigrants gravitate to Florida, New York, or Massachusetts.

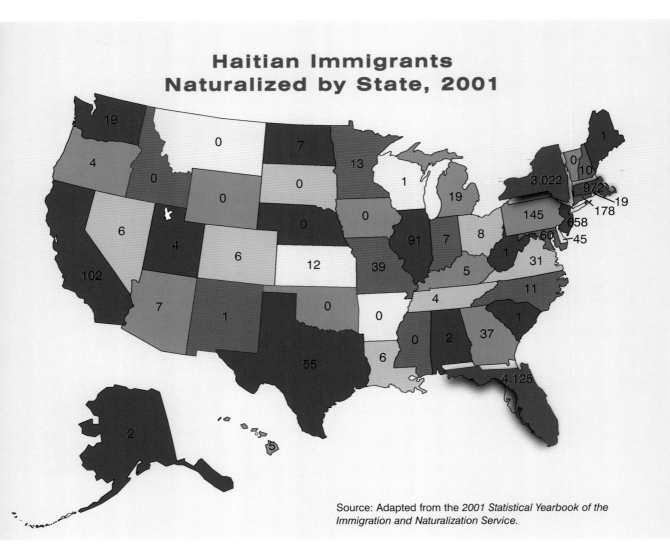

Haitian Immigrants Naturalized by State, 2001

Source: Adapted from the *2001 Statistical Yearbook of the Immigration and Naturalization Service.*

A grocery store in Miami's Little Haiti section. Miami, which boasts the largest Haitian American community in the United States, is home to more Haitians than any city in Haiti with the exception of Port-au-Prince.

they have the reputation of being the hardest working people in the Caribbean," Anthony Bryan, a University of Miami professor of international relations, told a Florida reporter in 2001. By the mid-1990s, the Miami area alone boasted more than 400 Haitian-owned businesses, and hundreds of smaller enterprises. The larger businesses have given the district of Little Haiti in North Miami its distinctive look. Many of these businesses have some connection to the local or overseas Haitian community. Among the most popular businesses are restaurants, grocery stores, travel agencies specializing in Caribbean trips, cargo shipping services, Haitian real estate agencies, and money exchanges.

The Growth of a Haitian American Identity

The Haitians who immigrated to North America in the 1960s, during the early years of the Duvalier regime, were largely middle-class professionals. Most believed their stay in the United States or Canada would be temporary—they intended to return to Haiti after Papa Doc was gone—and this explains why very few changed their citizenship. It probably also explains why, as a group, they took comparatively little interest in their communities in North America. Indeed, these early immigrants were frequently said to know more—and care more—about the political situation in Haiti than about problems with their local school system or city government.

However, as this generation matured and a new one prepared to take its place, a distinct Haitian American consciousness began to emerge. This was manifested in a rise in political and social activism, much of it directed toward improving the lot of recent immigrants. There was also a growing sense among members of the Haitian diaspora in the United States that their political voice could be brought to bear in pressuring the U.S. government to promote positive change in Haiti.

Not surprisingly, the centers of this growing Haitian American consciousness were the cities where the Haitian immigrant population was concentrated: Boston, Chicago, Philadelphia, and, especially, New York City and Miami (which by the 1980s had become the most popular destination for Haitians). In New York City, the National Democratic Party created a slot for Haitians on its All-American Council, which had previously consisted only of members of European ethnic groups. Shortly thereafter, the Haitian American Citizens Society was formed.

Another of New York's most active Haitian interest groups was the Haitian Refugee Center, established in the 1970s. This organization offered legal help to newly arrived immigrants and Haitian Americans. It also took an openly anti-Duvalier stance, denounced the military regimes that followed Jean-Claude Duvalier's departure, and opposed the coup that toppled the Aristide presidency.

Similar groups sprang up in Florida. In Miami, Combit Liberté—a political organization that opposed the Duvalier regime and was committed to protecting the rights and interests of Miami's Haitian population—appeared in 1978. After the fall of Jean-Claude Duvalier, the group changed its name to Veye Yo.

As the Haitian American community grew and came into its own, established institutions and government agencies began sponsoring programs designed to address the needs of Haitians. The Ford Foundation and the Catholic Church supported the creation and growth of Haitian community organizations. In areas with large Haitian populations, the Catholic Church also recruited Haitian priests to say Masses in Creole. Meanwhile, Protestant organizations such as the American Baptist Convention advocated the creation of individual Haitian congregations. And in 1975 the National Council of Churches established Haitian Refugee Concerns, an organization dedicated to helping immigrants and refugees.

During the 1970s, the New York City Development Agency funded separate Haitian community centers. Such centers were also established in other cities.

5 FITTING IN AND STANDING APART

When they arrive in North America, Haitians—like immigrants from all over the world—bring with them the culture of their homeland. The Creole language, strong communal and family values, an acquaintance with voodoo, and even certain foods all distinguish Haitians from other ethnic groups in North America.

Assimilation

The experiences of immigrant groups in North America, regardless of which region of the world they come from, generally follow a pattern. First-generation immigrants, particularly if they arrived in North America as adults, tend to retain many aspects of their original culture. And to a certain degree, this sets them apart from the mainstream. To cite one obvious example, many first-generation immigrants continue to speak their native tongue primarily or even exclusively, and the absence of English-language competency may limit their opportunities or even isolate them from the wider society. But the Canadian- or American-born children of first-generation immigrants typically do not have this difficulty. Even if their parents always speak another language at home, the children will learn English when they go to school. And they will also be exposed to North American attitudes and values, which in many cases differ from those common in their parents' homeland. Thus the

◀ Educational opportunities are limited in Haiti, but Haitian immigrants to the United States and Canada tend to make doing well in school a high priority for their children.

With second-generation Haitians, as with the children of other immigrants, school is a primary means of assimilation into North American culture.

second generation will almost inevitably be more assimilated into North American society than their parents. And members of the third or fourth generation will probably be completely at home in North American culture and, in fact, indistinguishable from native-born Americans or Canadians.

First-generation immigrants typically make considerable efforts to pass on their culture to their children. Again, using language as an example, immigrants often insist that their children learn their native tongue. In this respect, Haitians tend to differ from other immigrant groups. Haitians in North America generally do not insist that their children learn or speak Creole. In fact, many encourage their children to speak English like Americans do, believing that this will improve the children's prospects in life. Yet because most Haitians in the United States and Canada continue to maintain connections with their Creole-speaking relatives in Haiti, and because many just-comes arrive in North America without knowing English, there is reason to believe that even younger-generation Haitian Americans or Canadians will continue to know some Creole.

Generational Conflicts

As children reach adolescence and begin to assert their independence, some degree of conflict with their parents is almost inevitable. For immigrant families this conflict often centers on parents' expectations that their children will observe norms of behavior that were prevalent in their country of origin, and children's wishes to act more like their North American peers.

In Haiti, children are expected to respect their parents and obey without question. Yet among the children of Haitian immigrants in North America, complaints are frequently heard that parents are too strict. For example, Haitian parents typically insist that their teenage children be home before dark, and they often refuse to allow their daughters to date. Frequently, teenage Haitian Americans also chafe at the importance that their older relatives place upon "what people think." Girls in particular are closely monitored so that they will not embarrass the family. One second-generation Haitian commented:

> In Haiti, people are nosy [*tripot*]. That's the truth. I find Haitians to be nosy, they always want to mind other people's business. They do not understand the concept of privacy. For this reason, people always worry about *sa untel va di*? [what will so and so say?] Haitians have that mentality. To me, this is a problem. In the United States, people don't spend their time worrying about what others would say. . . . Many times, Haitian parents are more concerned about what their Haitian friends would say that about listening to their children. This is why they are so strict, they do not want their children to stay out late at night or to have some kind of freedom. If something goes wrong, their real fear has to do with "What would so and so say?"

Hiding One's Heritage

Many Haitians in North America have encountered prejudice, frequently because of mistaken beliefs about their culture. The sociologist Flore Zéphir describes a trend among some young Haitians to distance themselves from their Haitian background, usually in response to the prejudice that they encounter at school and in their neighborhood. Zéphir calls it the "undercover phenomenon." High school and sometimes even college students Anglicize their names and give false information about their pasts, claiming to be, in Zéphir's words, "anything but Haitian." Some say they are African, others from the Caribbean; those with accents might claim that they were raised in Canada or a French-speaking African country. By denying their background, the "undercovers" hope to avoid the labels and stereotypes directed against Haitians.

At the same time, the effort to conceal their heritage can create enormous stress and a sense of isolation, and if an "undercover" is exposed, the results can be devastating. In one particularly tragic case, a Haitian who had immigrated to the United States as a child and taken great pains to create an African American identity shot himself to death when a young relative spoke to him in Creole in front of his friends.

Divisions

Within the Haitian immigrant community, divisions exist that to some extent mirror the divisions within Haiti itself. Members of the more educated middle and upper classes often keep their distance from poorer, less educated immigrants. This can be seen, for example, in the distribution of Haitian American residences and businesses in South Florida. Most working-class and poor Haitians live in Miami's Little Haiti; by contrast, more established and affluent Haitian Americans make their homes and keep their businesses in the suburbs, and often they employ few, if any, fellow Haitians. Moreover, observers note that in the Haitian diaspora, as in Haiti, skin color continues to make a difference. Those with lighter skin tend to be from the privileged upper classes, and they and darker-skinned Haitians tend to view each other with suspicion.

Similarly, Haitians in the North American diaspora and Haitians who have remained on the island don't always see eye-to-eye. Although diaspora Haitians have pumped millions of dollars into Haiti's economy, and although they were steadfast supporters of Jean-Bertrand Aristide's first presidential campaign and his restoration to power, many in Haiti say that those living abroad have not done enough to improve conditions in their country. Diaspora Haitians who return to Haiti are sometimes disparaged as "*Kreyol touris*," or Creole tourists.

The Haitian American Media

One development that has brought Haitians together is the growth of the Haitian American media. Over the past 20 years, as the size of the diaspora community has increased, Haitian American media outlets have expanded their focus. Today they not only cover political developments in Haiti but also address the special interests and concerns of the Haitian community in the United States.

The flagship of the Haitian American press was the Creole-language *Haiti-Observateur*. Established in New York City in 1971, the year François Duvalier died, it spoke for many

A young boy displays the front page of *Haïti Progrès*. Founded in 1983 in New York City, the weekly features articles in English, French, and Creole and is distributed to the Haitian American communities in New York, Miami, Fort Lauderdale, Boston, Chicago, Philadelphia, and Washington, D.C. The newspaper also appears in Montreal and in Haiti.

Haitians in the area who had been driven from their country by the regime. After 1986, when Jean-Claude Duvalier went into exile, the *Haiti-Observateur* kept up a steady stream of criticism of Haiti's military regimes.

In 1983 a rival newspaper, the *Haïti Progrès*, made its debut in New York City. It was a paper that focused on social and economic issues, and it earned the reputation of being more left-wing than the *Haiti-Observateur*. *Haïti Progrès* was one of the earliest supporters of Jean-Bertrand Aristide.

Three years later, South Florida Haitians got their own long-overdue newspaper, *Haiti en Marche*. More so than its counterparts in New York City, *Haiti en Marche* featured a strong local focus. It covered topics that were of particular concern to the Haitians of South Florida, such as immigration and naturalization issues, candidates for local and state office, and events in the community.

The large Haitian American community of Boston is served by the *Haitian Reporter*. Founded in 2001, the English-language publication mixes local and Haitian news, editorials, and feature articles on a wide range of subjects, including politics, food, art and culture, and health care, employment, and immigration issues.

Radio stations have also served as a means of linking members of the Haitian community. All cities with large Haitian populations have at least one radio station that carries entertainment or educational programming geared to Haitians and Haitian Americans. Depending upon the character of the community, the programming may be in Creole, in English, or in both languages. Some stations have music and cultural programming; others schedule news and call-in shows. All of them advertise for Haitian-owned businesses or Haitian-oriented services.

More recently, the stations of South Florida have introduced emergency broadcasting in Creole, so that recent immigrants and Haitians who cannot read can be notified promptly in cases of natural disaster or crisis. Should a child disappear, a person with Alzheimer's wander off, or a gas leak require the evacuation of an area, a Creole-language emergency alert will help ensure that news reaches the Haitian population as soon as it reaches everyone else.

Religion

Spirituality is an integral part of Haitian life, and a high proportion of Haitians in North America continue to practice a religious faith. For example, in a survey of Haitian immigrants in South Florida, more than three-quarters described themselves as weekly churchgoers.

An estimated 80 percent of Haiti's population is Roman Catholic. While the majority of Haitians in North America are also Catholics, Protestantism has recently made inroads among the diaspora community. In South Florida, for example, up to 40 percent of the Haitians are members of a Protestant denomination.

6 PROBLEMS

Various factors have spurred Haitian immigration to North America. Poverty and political repression in Haiti pushed many to leave their homeland; the promise of freedom and economic opportunity pulled many to the United States and Canada. Many Haitians have realized their dreams of creating a better life for themselves and their children in North America. But many others have encountered unexpected problems and obstacles.

In the United States, race relations have historically been quite troubled, and it would be hard to deny that tensions continue to exist between black and white Americans. As blacks, many Haitian immigrants to the United States have found themselves the focus of racially based bigotry. But prejudice against Haitians has gone beyond skin color. Beginning in the 1980s, for example, Haitians were stigmatized by many people as "AIDS carriers." In addition, some Americans are afraid of and repulsed by the practice of voodoo, which is widespread in Haiti.

A Double Standard?

For their part, many in the Haitian community believe that discrimination against them sometimes extends to official government policies. In particular, Haitians—as well as immigration rights activists—have pointed to what they see as a double standard in U.S. immigration policy.

◀ Haitian Americans at this November 2002 demonstration in Miami are protesting the detention of 234 Haitian asylum-seekers whose boat ran aground at Key Biscayne. Over the years, many Haitians have complained about what they see as a double standard in the way the U.S. government treats Cuban and Haitian migrants.

A voodoo priestess, New Orleans. The spiritual practice of voodoo, widespread in Haiti, has been a source of prejudice against Haitian Americans.

From the early days of the Castro regime, Cubans who fled their country were routinely granted asylum in the United States. By contrast, Haitians fleeing their country at the same time were often denied asylum—even though the Duvaliers and the military regimes that followed were no less repressive than Castro. As a rule, during the Cold War the U.S. State Department defined people who had left Communist countries as political refugees (which gave them the right to asylum), whereas people from non-Communist countries were much more likely to be labeled economic migrants.

But Haitians, immigration activists, and human rights organizations suspected that this did not explain the disparity between the way Cuban refugees were treated and the way Haitian refugees were treated. These groups, along with the Congressional Black Caucus and the NAACP, contended that race was at the heart of the issue: almost 90 percent of Cubans are white or mulatto, whereas 95 percent of Haitians are black.

In July of 1980, Haitian refugees won their first legal battle when Judge James L. King ruled that the State Department's policy regarding Haitian and Cuban refugees was unconstitutional. Almost two decades later, the passage of the Haitian Refugee Immigration Fairness Act of 1998 (HRIFA) allowed Haitians who had applied for asylum or were paroled into the United States by December 31, 1995, to apply to become lawful permanent residents by April 1, 2000. Unfortunately, technical language in the bill was interpreted to exclude Haitians who arrived at ports of entry with false documents. Nevertheless, the act represented a significant legislative achievement and helped thousands of Haitians. As of March 31, 2003, the Bureau of Citizenship and Immigration Services had received 37,295 requests under HRIFA and had approved 9,555, according to the Government Accounting Office.

Yet such improvements in the treatment of Haitian asylum-seekers have, to a certain degree, been offset by other developments. On October 29, 2002, a 50-foot boat carrying more than 200 Haitian men, women, and children ran aground at Key Biscayne, Florida. Television cameras captured the image of people scrambling ashore and running onto a busy highway in hopes of avoiding capture. Although 40 of the refugees were granted bonds that guaranteed their release, the INS stopped the bonds from being issued on the grounds that the Haitians were a danger to national security. Protests from Haitian Americans and African Americans resulted in the release of two pregnant refugees on humanitarian grounds.

In the weeks that followed the landing, INS officials insisted that allowing the Haitians to remain free would open the door to a flood of refugees. Thousands more Haitians would endanger their own lives and interfere with the other responsibilities of the Coast Guard in the region, the INS claimed.

Controversy in New York

New York City, home to the oldest Haitian settlement in the United States, was the site of two recent events that served as a catalyst for the political mobilization of the Haitian American community. On August 9, 1997, white New York City police

Haitian immigrant Abner Louima (left) with his lawyer Johnnie Cochran. In 1997 Louima was brutally assaulted by New York City police officers. The incident galvanized the Haitian American community.

officers arrested a Haitian immigrant named Abner Louima outside a nightclub. While handcuffed, Louima was beaten en route to the police precinct. There the attack continued, as a group of officers punched, kicked, and assaulted Louima, causing serious injuries. All the while, the officers taunted him with racial insults. When the incident came to light, Haitians—along with Americans of all races and nationalities—were stunned and outraged by the brutality of the police officers' actions.

A second high-profile incident involving New York City police officers and a member of the Haitian community occurred three years later, in 2000. In that case a plainclothes officer fatally shot Patrick Dorismond, an unarmed Haitian American man, in disputed circumstances. New York's mayor, Rudolph Giuliani, quickly labeled the shooting justified and released Dorismond's sealed juvenile criminal records, angering the dead man's family and Haitian community leaders. The already strained relations between Haitians and New York police and city officials further deteriorated during Dorismond's funeral procession. Haitian custom requires mourners to touch the casket or the hearse of the deceased as it proceeds to the cemetery. When thousands of Haitians surged into the streets during the funeral procession, police moved in, perhaps believing that a riot was about to break out. A melee ensued, during which more than 20 police officers were injured and several dozen Haitian Americans were arrested.

The Dorismond and Louima cases spurred Haitian American leaders to organize their community in an effort to force government and law enforcement officials to examine, and ultimately take steps to improve, the way Haitians and Haitian Americans are treated. In this effort New York's Haitian and African American communities forged alliances that, many hoped, would provide the basis for more effective political action.

7 THE FUTURE

By the early years of the 21st century, Haitians had established a significant presence in North America. The 2000 U.S. census counted more than 548,000 people of Haitian ancestry, up from about 300,000 only 10 years before. Meanwhile, Canada's 2001 census counted more than 52,000 Haitian immigrants. Particularly in the United States, the actual numbers may be significantly higher because of undocumented migrants who were not counted in the census.

Bleak Prospects

During the first large wave of Haitian immigration to North America, in the 1960s, the immigrants tended to view their stay in the United States or Canada as temporary. When conditions in Haiti improved, many thought, they would return to the land of their birth.

But today, four decades later, Haiti remains politically torn, and economic and social conditions are dismal. By 2003 many Haitians in the United States, surveying the current state of affairs on the island, had concluded that they would not be returning anytime soon, if ever. They saw a nation whose president, once a hero of democracy and a champion of justice, seemed to have adopted an increasingly autocratic stance, a leader who failed to speak out or take action when his critics were murdered. They saw a nation whose cities were being

◀ If current trends continue, a significant proportion of today's Haitian children will find a future not in the country of their birth, but in North America.

terrorized by well-armed gangs committing a variety of crimes and dispensing "street justice"—and the government would not, or could not, put an end to it. They saw a poverty rate of 80 percent. They saw an economy that could not offer Haiti's people jobs and the prospect of a decent standard of living. They heard a litany of depressing health statistics: For every 1,000 babies born in Haiti, 79 will die before their first birthday. Overall life expectancy is just 51. An estimated 250,000 Haitians—more than 6 percent of the adult population—have AIDS or are infected with the virus that causes it.

A Voice Stilled by Violence

Jean Dominique was born into a privileged mulatto family in 1931, but he was raised to identify with the plight of Haiti's poor blacks. As a young man, Dominique joined rural development projects and studied at the Haitian Agricultural School. After graduating from the University of Paris, he returned to Haiti, where he taught impoverished rural farmers and residents of the urban slums how to better grow crops.

Dominique's family quickly made enemies in the first Duvalier government. One of his brothers was killed while trying to overthrow the regime. Jean Dominique was arrested and tortured because President Duvalier believed that he had been involved. After a month, he was released, and he soon accepted a job at Radio Haiti. Two years later he bought the station and turned it into an anti-Duvalier organ.

On November 28, 1980, the Tonton Macoutes destroyed the radio station. Dominique escaped to New York, where he lived until the collapse of Jean-Claude Duvalier's government. A stream of small donations from Haitians around the world financed the reconstruction of Radio Haiti, which resumed its pro-democracy activities in 1986.

In 1991 President Jean-Bertrand Aristide asked Jean Dominique to become his Minister of Information, but the journalist refused, preferring to remain outside politics. Soon Radio Haiti became a target of the same forces that overthrew Aristide. Dominique and his family fled to New York, where they remained until 1994. After returning to Haiti, Dominique rebuilt his radio station. But on April 3, 2000, he was murdered by gunmen when he arrived at work. The killers were never apprehended.

Haitian children line up for class at a shelter for AIDS orphans near Port-au-Prince. More than 6 percent of all Haitian adults are thought to have AIDS or be infected with HIV, the virus that causes the deadly disease.

The Immigration Solution

If circumstances like these are likely to deter most Haitians in North America from returning to Haiti, at least for the foreseeable future, they are also likely to drive more and more Haitians to leave their homeland. Immigration—whether legal or illegal—will be seen by many as the best solution to the terrible problems created by their country's continuing decline.

Given the abundant political freedoms and economic opportunities that exist in North America, a significant number of Haitians will no doubt continue to make Canada and, especially, the United States their destination. And family-oriented

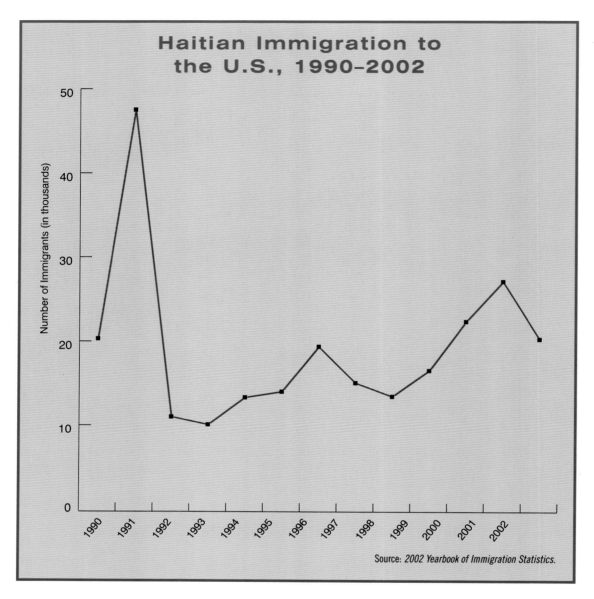

Haitian Immigration to the U.S., 1990–2002

Source: *2002 Yearbook of Immigration Statistics.*

Haitians in North America will contribute to this trend by working hard to help relatives immigrate.

Large Haitian enclaves, complete with well-established businesses and social and cultural organizations, exist in a number of North American cities. Boston, New York City, and Miami are each home to more Haitians than any city in Haiti with the exception of Port-au-Prince. And with Haiti's economy in a shambles, these cities have assumed a role as primary centers of

Haitian immigration has fluctuated with the political climate, but as of 2002 Haiti remained among the top 15 source countries for immigrants to the United States.

Haitian economic and commercial activity.

As the 21st century unfolds, third-, fourth-, and fifth-generation Haitian Americans will become fully assimilated into U.S. society, a process that occurs with all immigrant groups. Yet even if their knowledge of Haitian culture and the Creole language fades, these diaspora Haitians will remain key to any hopes that their ancestral land can one day emerge as a stable, prosperous society.

FAMOUS HAITIAN AMERICANS/CANADIANS

Jean-Michel Basquiat (1960–1988), a Haitian American painter, was born on December 2, 1960, in Brooklyn, New York. His father, Gerard, belonged to a prominent family that President François Duvalier had forced into exile.

Basquiat had a troubled family life. His parents divorced when he was seven, and his father, a very strict disciplinarian, was awarded custody of the couple's children. As a teenager, Basquiat frequently ran away, living in the streets or parks of New York City. He also began to take drugs.

Basquiat attended the City-as-School, but he dropped out after hitting the principal in the face with a pie during a graduation ceremony. Basquiat spent all of his time painting images and slogans around Manhattan. He became friends with the artist Keith Haring and a protégé of Andy Warhol.

By the 1980s, Basquiat was a rising star in the New York art world. One critic claimed that his paintings "represented the chaos of the black man within the dysfunctional American dream." But as his reputation grew, so did his addiction to cocaine and heroin. In August of 1988, Jean-Michel Basquiat died of a drug overdose.

Edwidge Danticat (1969–   ), an acclaimed writer, was born in Port-au-Prince. At the age of 12, she immigrated to the United States, joining her parents, who had immigrated earlier, in Brooklyn, New York. Before this time she had not spoken English, but within two years of her arrival in the United States Danticat was publishing stories about the immigration and diaspora experience in the local newspaper. The history of Haiti, emigration, and family relationships would become important themes in her novels.

After majoring in French literature at Barnard College in New York, Danticat earned a Master of Fine Arts degree from Brown University. She now teaches creative writing at New York University. Her novels, *Breath, Eyes, Memory* and *The Farming of Bones*, and her collection of short stories, *Krik Krak!* have been translated into more than a dozen languages. Since 1994 she has won the Pushcart Short Story Prize, the Best Young American Novelist Award, the American Book Award, and the International Flaino Prize for Literature.

Wyclef Jean (1972–   ), a musician, producer, and hip-hop artist, was born in Croix-des-Bouquets, Haiti, but moved with his family to Brooklyn, New York, at the age of nine.

As a teenager, he became interested in music. In 1987 Jean—along with his cousin Prakazrel Michel and a classmate of Michel's, Lauryn Hill—formed a rap group. As the Fugees, the trio won critical and popular success with their second album, *The Score*. Released in 1996, it has sold more than 6 million copies worldwide.

Jean has also had a successful solo career, beginning with 1997's *The Carnival*. In addition, he has produced the records of various hip-hop, pop, and R&B artists.

Prakazrel "Pras" Michel (1972–   ), a Haitian American songwriter, music producer, and actor, was born and raised in New Jersey. With high school classmate Lauryn Hill and cousin Wyclef Jean, he formed the Fugees, a group that stormed the pop charts with the 1996 release *The Score*.

In addition to various solo music projects and work as a producer, Michel has found time to appear in motion pictures, including *Mystery Men* (1999) and *Turn It Up* (2000).

Marie St. Fleur (1962–   ) became the first Haitian American elected to a state legislature when, in 1999, she won a seat in the Massachusetts House of Representatives. St. Fleur, a Democrat, represents the Fifth Suffolk District, which includes parts of Boston. She is chairperson of the Committee on Education, Arts and Humanities.

Born in Haiti, St. Fleur came to the United States at the age of seven, when her family fled the regime of François Duvalier. Before entering politics, she attended the University of Massachusetts at Amherst, then obtained a law degree from Boston College Law School. She served in the district attorney's office of Middlesex County and, later, as an assistant attorney general of Massachusetts.

GLOSSARY

acquired immune deficiency syndrome (AIDS)—a fatal blood-borne disease, caused by a virus that attacks the human immune system. When the disease was first identified in the early 1980s, it was wrongly associated with Haitians.

African swine flu—a contagious disease that spread from Africa to the Western Hemisphere in the late 1970s. In order to keep the disease from reaching the United States and Canada, the Haitian government was pressured to launch a campaign to kill all of the pigs in the country, with disastrous social and economic results.

Arawaks—the indigenous people who lived on the island of Hispaniola before European settlement, and who named it Ayti. Within the Arawak are the Taino and Carib tribes.

boat people—a term coined in the late 1970s, referring to refugees from Haiti and Cuba who sailed to the United States, usually in freighters or small craft.

Creole—the Haitian language, which combines Arawak, Spanish, African, and French structures and vocabulary.

deforestation—the removal of trees and forest cover by human or natural means.

diaspora—a community of people who belong to a nation or country, but who do not live within that country.

houngan—a voodoo priest.

interdiction—the interception or cutting off of; specifically, the policy permitting U.S. Coast Guard cutters to apprehend, on the high seas, Haitians attempting to enter the United States illegally.

just-come—the Creole term for Haitians who have recently immigrated to the United States.

mambo—a voodoo priestess.

mulatto—a Haitian of African and European descent.

remittances—money or goods that diaspora Haitians send to their family members in Haiti.

GLOSSARY

Tonton Macoutes—nickname of the Volunteers for National Security (VSN), a much-hated force set up by, and loyal to, François Duvalier.

undercover—a Haitian, usually young, who tries to conceal his or her Haitian background from friends, acquaintances, and class-mates.

voodoo—a religion, practiced by most Haitians, that combines ele-ments of Arawak, African, and Christian spiritual beliefs. Voodoo teaches that spirits of the ancestors are active in the world and may be summoned during ceremonies.

yaws—a disfiguring disease that is found in places where water is stagnant and people walk barefoot. Symptoms of the disease are lesions, or sores on the body, and the gradual disintegra-tion of ears, lips, and nose.

FURTHER READING

Abbott, Elizabeth. *Haiti: The Duvaliers and Their Legacy.* New York: McGraw-Hill, 1989.

Aristide, Jean-Bertrand. *Dignity*, trans. Carrol F. Coates. Charlottesville: University Press of Virginia, 1996.

————. *Eyes of the Heart: Seeking a Path for the Poor in the Age of Globalization*, ed. Laura Flynn. Monroe, Maine: Common Courage Press, 2000.

Cadet, Robert. *Restavec: From Haitian Slave Child to Middle-Class American.* Austin: University of Texas Press, 1998.

Danticat, Edwidge, *Behind the Mountains: The Diary of Celiane Espérance.* New York: Orchard Books, 2001.

————. *Breath, Eyes, Memory.* New York: Soho Press, 1994.

————. *The Farming of Bones: A Novel.* New York: Soho Press, 1998.

————. *Krik! Krak!* New York: Soho Press, 1995.

————, ed. *The Butterfly's Way: Voices from the Haitian Dyaspora in the United States.* New York: Soho Press, 2001.

Haggerty, Richard, A., ed. *Dominican Republic and Haiti.* Washington, D.C.: Federal Research Division, Library of Congress, 1989.

Hoban, Phoebe. *Basquiat: A Quick Killing in Art.* New York: Viking, 1998.

Laguerre, Michel S. *Haitian Americans in Transnational America.* New York: St. Martin's Press, 1998.

Pamphile, Léon. *Haitians and African Americans: A Heritage of Tragedy and Hope.* Gainesville: University Press of Florida, 2001.

FURTHER READING

Schiller, Nina Glick, and Georges Eugene Fouron. *Georges Woke Up Laughing: Long-Distance Nationalism and the Search for Home.* Durham, N.C.: Duke University Press, 2001.

Shacochis, Bob. *The Immaculate Invasion.* New York: Viking, 1999.

Stepick, Alex. *Pride Against Prejudice: Haitians in the United States.* Boston: Allyn and Bacon, 1998.

Zéphir, Flore. *Trends in Ethnic Identification Among Second-Generation Haitian Immigrants in New York City.* Westport, Conn.: Bergin & Garvey, 2001.

INTERNET RESOURCES

http://www.aristidefoundation.haiti.org/
Aristide Foundation for Democracy. This website describes the goals and projects of Jean-Bertrand Aristide.

http://www.cic.gc.ca/english
Citizenship and Immigration Canada.

http://www.haiti.org
Website of the Republic of Haiti's embassy in Washington, D.C.

http://www.haitiantimes.com
This is the website of the Boston-based newspaper the *Haitian Times*.

http://www.nchr.org
The National Coalition for Haitian Rights is active in issues pertaining to immigration and the political and social interests of Haitians in the United States.

http://ucis.gov/graphics/index.htm
Website of the U.S. Citizenship and Immigration Services.

http://www.uhhp.com
The United Haitians Home Page is a clearinghouse of information about Haitian communities in the United States and Haiti.

Publisher's Note: The websites listed on this page were active at the time of publication. The publisher is not responsible for websites that have changed their address or discontinued operation since the date of publication. The publisher reviews and updates the websites each time the book is reprinted.

Numbers in **bold italic** refer to captions.

Index

INDEX

CONTRIBUTORS

SENATOR EDWARD M. KENNEDY has represented Massachusetts in the United States Senate for more than 40 years. Kennedy serves on the Senate Judiciary Committee, where he is the senior Democrat on the Immigration Subcommittee. He currently is the ranking member on the Health, Education, Labor and Pensions Committee in the Senate, and also serves on the Armed Services Committee, where he is a member of the Senate Arms Control Observer Group. He is also a member of the Congressional Friends of Ireland and a trustee of the John F. Kennedy Center for the Performing Arts in Washington, D.C.

Throughout his career, Kennedy has fought for issues that benefit the citizens of Massachusetts and the nation, including the effort to bring quality health care to every American, education reform, raising the minimum wage, defending the rights of workers and their families, strengthening the civil rights laws, assisting individuals with disabilities, fighting for cleaner water and cleaner air, and protecting and strengthening Social Security and Medicare for senior citizens.

Kennedy is the youngest of nine children of Joseph P. and Rose Fitzgerald Kennedy, and is a graduate of Harvard University and the University of Virginia Law School. His home is in Hyannis Port, Massachusetts, where he lives with his wife, Victoria Reggie Kennedy, and children, Curran and Caroline. He also has three grown children, Kara, Edward Jr., and Patrick, and four grandchildren.

Senior consulting editor STUART ANDERSON served as Executive Associate Commissioner for Policy and Planning and Counselor to the Commissioner at the Immigration and Naturalization Service from August 2001 until January 2003. He spent four and a half years on Capitol Hill on the Senate Immigration Subcommittee, first for Senator Spencer Abraham and then as Staff Director of the subcommittee for Senator Sam Brownback. Prior to that, he was Director of Trade and Immigration Studies at the Cato Institute in Washington, D.C., where he produced reports on the history of immigrants in the military and the role of immigrants in high technology. He currently serves as Executive Director of the National Foundation for American Policy, a nonpartisan public policy research organization focused on trade, immigration, and international relations. He has an M.A. from Georgetown University and a B.A. in Political Science from Drew University. His articles have appeared in such publications as the *Wall Street Journal*, *New York Times*, and *Los Angeles Times*.

MARIAN L. SMITH served as the senior historian of the U.S. Immigration and Naturalization Service (INS) from 1988 to 2003, and is currently the immigration and naturalization historian within the Department of Homeland Security in Washington, D.C. She studies, publishes, and speaks on the history of the immigration agency and is active in the management of official 20th-century immigration records.

PETER HAMMERSCHMIDT is the First Secretary (Financial and Military Affairs) for the Permanent Mission of Canada to the United Nations. Before taking this position, he was a ministerial speechwriter and policy specialist for the Department of National

Defence in Ottawa. Prior to joining the public service, he served as the Publications Director for the Canadian Institute of Strategic Studies in Toronto. He has a B.A. (Honours) in Political Studies from Queen's University, and an MScEcon in Strategic Studies from the University of Wales, Aberystwyth. He currently lives in New York, where in his spare time he operates a freelance editing and writing service, Wordschmidt Communications.

Manuscript reviewer ESTHER OLAVARRIA serves as General Counsel to Senator Edward M. Kennedy, ranking Democrat on the U.S. Senate Judiciary Committee, Subcommittee on Immigration. She is Senator Kennedy's primary advisor on immigration, nationality, and refugee legislation and policies. Prior to her current job, she practiced immigration law in Miami, Florida, working at several nonprofit organizations. She cofounded the Florida Immigrant Advocacy Center and served as managing attorney, supervising the direct service work of the organization and assisting in the advocacy work. She also worked at Legal Services of Greater Miami, as the directing attorney of the American Immigration Lawyers Association Pro Bono Project, and at the Haitian Refugee Center, as a staff attorney. She clerked for a Florida state appellate court after graduating from the University of Florida Law School. She was born in Havana, Cuba, and raised in Florida.

Reviewer JANICE V. KAGUYUTAN is Senator Edward M. Kennedy's advisor on immigration, nationality, and refugee legislation and policies. Prior to working on Capitol Hill, Ms. Kaguyutan was a staff attorney at the NOW Legal Defense and Education Fund's Immigrant Women Program. Ms. Kaguyutan has written and trained extensively on the rights of immigrant victims of domestic violence, sexual assault, and human trafficking. Her previous work includes representing battered immigrant women in civil protection order, child support, divorce, and custody hearings, as well as representing immigrants before the Immigration and Naturalization Service on a variety of immigration matters.

JENA M. GAINES was born in Newport, Rhode Island. She studied cultural anthropology at Mount Holyoke College and Bridgewater State College. She earned an M.A. and Ph.D. in History from the University of Virginia.

PICTURE CREDITS